THE
WOMAN'S DAY
FOOD PROCESSOR
COOKBOOK

THE WOMAN'S DAY FOOD PROCESSOR COOKBOOK

by

Marjorie Page Blanchard

Fawcett Columbine • New York

THE WOMAN'S DAY FOOD PROCESSOR COOKBOOK

Published by Fawcett Columbine Books, CBS Educational and Professional Publishing, a division of CBS Inc.

ISBN: 0-449-90062-2

Plates 2, 3, 4, 5, 6, and 7 are by Woman's Day Studio

All other photos by Robert H. Epstein

Printed in the United States of America

First Fawcett Columbine printing: November 1981

10 9 8 7 6 5 4 3 2 1

CONTENTS

INTRODUCTION

Here, at last, is a food processor cookbook designed for your everyday cooking needs. It was written especially for people who want to save time, energy and money as they prepare three meals a day and snacks in between, but who still want flavorful, nutritious dishes that their family and friends will enjoy. Not only are the basics turned out in seconds (40 seconds for a pie shell, 30 seconds for a loaf of bread, 20 seconds for a batch of cookies, 10 seconds for a meat loaf) but there will be added excitement in the creation of new dishes such as Eggplant on the Half Shell, Zucchini-Walnut Soufflé, Stuffed Potato Pancake, Apple-Banana Crumble, Cheesy Brioche Loaf and Chocolate Cream Puffs with Peppermint Filling.

If time seems in short supply these days as we rush from one job to another, we should stretch it out as much as we can—and the food processor helps. It also stretches out the food supply as we recycle leftovers into patties, loaves and fillings for pasta shells or pancakes. Once you get the technique of using this machine to its fullest capacities, there will be no waste of time or materials. This book is designed to show you how to fit the food processor into your daily life so it actually speeds up and smooths out the time spent in meal making—as well as letting you have fun doing it.

In addition to saving time, we all want to know how to get the best value from our food, in terms of both health and money. Here again the processor comes into its own. With the instantaneous chopping, grinding and grating mechanisms, the processor will actually encourage you to use more fresh vegetables, make more salads and serve more vegetable main dishes. Vegetables have never looked so good!

As far as economy goes, there is much less waste because a lot of food can be recycled. Hearty soups are one of the best ways to feed a family and keep them healthy and happy, and soup making is one of the things this machine does best—out of leftovers, of course. Sprinkle a homemade soup with lots of grated cheese, serve it with homemade bread and a fruit pie, and you become the Mother or Father of the Year.

7

You can also save on meat, because a little goes a long way when it is ground or chopped and combined with puréed vegetables as fillings for chicken breasts, quiches and crepes. You will also find yourself automatically grinding up bits and pieces (cheeses, stale bread, ends of roasts) to freeze for future use.

In this book we have tried to cover everything from brown-bag snacks to holiday feasting, with a whole year of just plain cooking and eating in between. We believe that fitting the food processor into your daily routine is just a matter of habit, and once you get the habit you'll say to yourself, "How did I ever get along without it?" To start you off easily we have put together a lesson on getting acquainted with the food processor. After you have thoroughly studied the instruction book that comes with your machine, take our lesson. When you have finished it, you will not only have used all of the blades many times and learned a lot of basic techniques, but you will also have produced an excellent five-course dinner. And you should be very proud of yourself.

USE OF THE FOOD PROCESSOR

In testing the recipes for this book we worked on eight different machines. They were of various shapes and sizes but all worked on the same basic principle with the same types of blades.

The heights of the workbowls are the same in most machines. They are all 4 inches, except for a Cuisinart model that is 5 inches.

All machines have an on-off button and a pulse button.

The feed tubes vary slightly in diameter.

The main difference in the machines we used is in the power of the motor and the resultant power in performance. Some are belt driven, some are direct drive. The less powerful machines do not chop or grate hard foods as easily as the stronger machines. However, even the smallest machine will make a good loaf of bread. As we could not test each recipe eight times, we have given an average time for processing or pulsing. You go from there, working it out with your own machine. The secret is to go *slowly*, and there will be less chance of overprocessing. Also *pay attention*. This is not a machine you can go off and leave to "do its own thing."

All processors come with 3 or 4 blades. You will use the METAL BLADE most frequently. It chops, grates, grinds, minces and crumbs. The desired texture of the food can be controlled by the bursts of speed that you use. When in doubt, use the pulse button.

The PLASTIC BLADE will be used the least, but it is good for mixing soft foods such as cream cheese to be used in spreads or dips.

The SHREDDING DISC can be controlled by the pressure you put on the food as you push it into the feed tube. *Always* use the plastic pusher.

The SLICING DISC should also be controlled this way. Most of the slicing discs have serrated edges. Always use a serrated blade for slicing meat.

There are accessory attachments for some machines and, as time goes on, there will be more. Be sure you see them demonstrated before you invest in any of these attachments. Ask yourself, Will I use this enough to justify the purchase?

Following are some helpful hints:
• Start slowly. Do not overprocess.
• Limit the amount of liquid you add, to slightly under the machine's capacity. When in doubt, process in two batches.
• Do not overload.
• Place material to be processed evenly around bowl.
• If a vegetable or fruit will not fit into the top of the feed tube, try putting it in from the bottom—which, in most machines, is slightly larger in diameter.
• Cut material to be processed into equal-size pieces. The end results will be evenly shaped and sized.
• Most foods will process better if they are chilled. Cheeses and meats *must* be chilled.
• Always use fresh ingredients. Tired fruits and vegetables will come out tired.
• Remember that processors differ in their abilities. What may take five seconds on one machine could be three or seven seconds on another. You learn through practice, and getting to know your own machine. The timing suggestions in these recipes are flexible.
• The most efficient way to use the processor is to assemble your ingredients ahead in their various stages of preparation. Cube the meat, dice the cheese, cut vegetables into lengths, etc. Place them all on the counter near the processor, with necessary cooking equipment close by.
• Process your ingredients in the order that will save cleanup. The general rule is dry ingredients first, wet ingredients second.
• Convert your favorite recipes to use in the processor. To do this you need not rewrite the recipe in its entirety; just number the ingredients in the order in which they will be processed. Write down next to the ingredient what the necessary preparation will be. After you have run through the recipe once, note down how many seconds each ingredient takes to process.
• To get the most out of your processor, make up batches of basics in quantity (grated cheese, bread crumbs, chopped parsley, herb butters, chopped mushrooms, soup bases) and freeze them.

Finally, remember that you control the machine, it does not control you.

Select tomatoes small enough to fit feed tube.
Insert through bottom of tube.

Remove stem end of tomatoes before slicing.

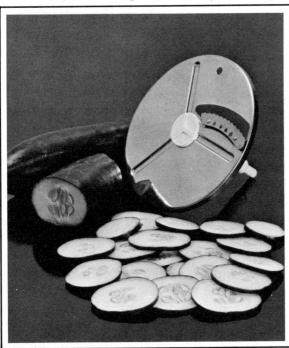

Cucumber slices for salad or garnish.

Stack zucchini in feed tube
horizontally for shredding.

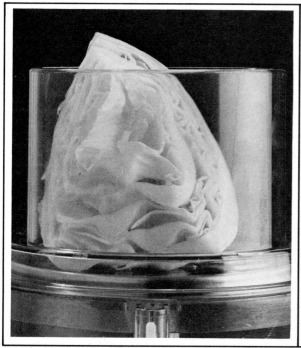

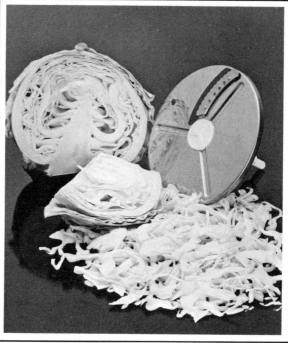

Cabbage wedge positioned for shredding or slicing.

Use slicing disc to shred cabbage coarsely.

Remove ends from potatoes for slicing.

Stack mushrooms sideways in tube. Slice with firm pressure.

Shred chilled, firm cheese.

Chill pepperoni before slicing.

Roll seeded peppers tightly
and pack upright in tube.

Cut root end off onion for slicing.

Pack celery pieces tightly in tube for slicing.

Stack apple quarters sides down
in tube for slicing.

Chop nuts with metal blade.

Halve orange lengthwise for slicing.

A LESSON

Getting Acquainted with the Food Processor

MENU

Beef-and-Mushroom Dip

Cream of Broccoli Soup

Pork and Sweet Potato Roulade

Corn Custards

Sliced Apple-Celery Salad

Homemade Mayonnaise

*Buttermilk Banana Cake
with Pecan Butter Cream Icing*

BEEF-AND-MUSHROOM DIP

With crispy chips or crackers, this dip makes a good opener for any meal.

1 2½-ounce jar dried beef
1 green onion, sliced
4–5 mushrooms, quartered
2 tablespoons parsley, stems removed

2 3-ounce packages cream cheese with chives, cut in 1-inch cubes
Freshly ground pepper
2 drops hot pepper sauce

Fit processor with METAL BLADE. Separate slices of beef and arrange around inside of processor bowl. Sprinkle onion over beef. Lock cover on. Process 5 seconds, until finely chopped. Add mushrooms. Process 5 seconds. Replace METAL BLADE with PLASTIC BLADE. Add parsley and cream cheese. Process 10 seconds until mixture is smooth, scraping down from sides if necessary. Add pepper and hot pepper sauce. Process 2 seconds. Remove mixture with rubber spatula to 3-cup ovenproof dish. Bake in preheated 350° oven for 20 minutes. Serve with crackers or chips. Makes 6 servings.

CREAM OF BROCCOLI SOUP

1 small onion, quartered
1 medium rib celery, cut in 1-inch lengths
1½ cups frozen, chopped broccoli (10-ounce package)
3 tablespoons butter or margarine

3 tablespoons flour
2 cups chicken bouillon
1 cup half-and-half
Salt to taste
Freshly ground pepper
½ teaspoon ground nutmeg

Fit processor with METAL BLADE. Arrange onion and celery pieces evenly around processor bowl. Fit on cover and lock. Turn switch to ON and process for 4 seconds. Turn OFF. Remove cover and blade. With rubber spatula, remove vegetables to saucepan. Add broccoli to saucepan. Cover with boiling salted water. Cook until vegetables are very soft. Do not wash processor bowl. Fit with METAL BLADE. Strain cooked vegetables into processor bowl. Process 10 seconds, until mixture is smooth but not runny—there should be some texture. Stop motor. Remove cover and blade. With spatula, remove contents to saucepan. Without washing bowl, add butter, flour and chicken bouillon. Replace METAL BLADE. Process 5 seconds, until smooth. Add to saucepan. Bring to a boil, stirring. When soup is thick and smooth, stir in half-and-half and seasonings. Serve hot. Makes 6 6-ounce servings. This may be made ahead and reheated, but do not boil again.

PORK AND SWEET POTATO ROULADE

1 pound sweet potatoes or yams
1 slice bread, torn up
½ pound boneless lean pork, cut in ½-inch cubes
1 1-pound chicken breast, skinned, boned, cut in ½-inch cubes
1 egg
½ medium onion, quartered
Salt to taste
Freshly ground pepper

2 tablespoons parsley, stems removed
¼ teaspoon ground nutmeg
2 tablespoons brown sugar, packed
2 strips orange peel, 1 inch x ½ inch
½ teaspoon ground ginger
2 tablespoons melted butter or margarine
1 orange, peeled and sliced

Cook potatoes in boiling salted water until very tender. Fit processor with METAL BLADE. Put bread into processor bowl. Process 5 seconds, until crumbs are fine. Remove to small bowl. Without washing bowl, arrange pork and chicken cubes evenly in it. Process 5 seconds. If there are any large pieces remaining, use pulse button 2 to 3 times until all meat is finely ground. Add egg, onion, salt, pepper, parsley and nutmeg. Pulse 4 to 5 times. Add crumbs. Pulse 3 to 4 times. Do not overmix. Remove mixture to large piece of waxed paper. Pat or roll out into a rectangle approximately 8 x 10 inches. Remove blade and wash processor bowl. Replace METAL BLADE. Process brown sugar and orange peel 10 seconds. Peel cooked potatoes and cut into chunks. Add to processor bowl with ginger. Process 10 to 15 seconds until smooth, stopping machine to scrape down sides if necessary. Spread potato mixture over meat. Lift waxed paper and roll up meat, starting at the long side. Roll onto lightly greased baking sheet. Bake in preheated 350° oven for 45 minutes. Cool. Cut into 1-inch slices and arrange on oven-proof platter. Before serving, sprinkle with melted butter and garnish with orange slices. Reheat in 350° oven for 20 minutes. Makes 6 servings.

CORN CUSTARDS

1½ cups corn kernels, fresh, or 10-ounce package, frozen
½ cup parsley, stems removed
4 eggs
1 teaspoon prepared mustard

½ teaspoon salt
Freshly ground pepper
1 teaspoon sugar
2–3 drops hot pepper sauce
1½ cups light cream

If corn is frozen, put kernels into sieve and run hot water through them until separated. Fit processor with METAL BLADE. Process parsley 10 seconds. Remove. Add corn and eggs to processor bowl. Process 15 seconds, until mixture is fairly smooth; it will still have texture. Add remaining ingredients and process 3 seconds. Remove blade. Pour mixture into well-greased 2½-inch muffin or custard cups. Fill to the top. Place cups in pan of hot water and cover loosely with foil. Place in preheated 375° oven and bake for 25 to 30 minutes, until firm and puffy. Remove cups from water and let stand 10 minutes. Run knife around edges and turn out onto serving platter. Surround each custard with chopped parsley. These may be made ahead and reheated on an ovenproof platter. Makes 10 to 12 custards.

SLICED APPLE-CELERY SALAD

½ cup walnuts
1 small carrot, scraped, cut in 2-inch lengths
6 medium stalks celery, cut in 2-inch lengths

3 medium apples, cored and quartered
Homemade Mayonnaise (recipe follows)

Fit processor with METAL BLADE. Turn nuts into processor bowl. Pulse 4 to 5 times until finely chopped. Turn out. Replace METAL BLADE with SHREDDING DISC. Stand up lengths of carrot in feed tube. Apply moderate pressure with pusher and shred carrot. Remove. Replace SHREDDING DISC with SLICING DISC. Stand up celery stalks in feed tube. Apply moderate pressure with pusher and slice celery. Stack apple quarters in feed tube, cut sides down. Apply moderate pressure with pusher and slice. Don't be discouraged if the slices are uneven; making them even takes a little practice. Remove vegetables to salad bowl. Wipe out processor bowl. Fit with METAL BLADE. Make dressing.

HOMEMADE MAYONNAISE

1 egg
2 teaspoons lemon juice
1 teaspoon salt

Freshly ground pepper
½ teaspoon dry mustard
1½ cups oil

Put egg, lemon juice, salt, pepper and mustard in bowl. Add ½ cup oil. Process 2 seconds. With motor running, add remaining oil very slowly in thin stream through the feed tube. When all oil has been added, mixture should have thickened. Makes 1½ cups. *To serve salad:* toss apples and celery with enough mayonnaise to moisten. Sprinkle nuts and carrot over top. Makes 6 servings.

BUTTERMILK PECAN-BANANA CAKE

2 cups flour
1 teaspoon baking powder
¾ teaspoon baking soda
½ teaspoon salt
1 cup pecans
2 medium ripe bananas, cut in
    1-inch lengths

½ cup butter or margarine
½ cup brown sugar, packed
1 teaspoon vanilla
2 eggs
½ cup buttermilk
Pecan Butter Cream Icing
    (recipe follows)

Combine ½ cup flour with baking powder, soda and salt. Set aside. Fit processor with METAL BLADE. Add pecans to processor bowl. Pulse 4 to 5 times, using short bursts of speed. Nuts should be quite finely chopped, but do not overchop or they will become oily and pasty. Remove to small bowl. Without washing processor bowl, add bananas. Process 5 to 6 seconds, until well mashed, stopping machine to scrape down sides if necessary. Add butter and brown sugar. Process 30 seconds, until mixture is quite smooth with no large lumps of butter. You may have to process 10 seconds longer. Leave motor running and remove plunger from feed tube. Add vanilla, eggs and buttermilk through feed tube. Process 3 to 4 seconds. Turn off machine. Remove cover and add 1½ cups flour. Process 6 to 7 seconds, until flour is mixed in. Add ½ cup chopped pecans and remaining ½ cup flour mixture. Pulse 4 to 5 times. Flour will still show slightly on top of batter and batter will look bubbly. With rubber spatula, turn out into greased 9-inch baking pan. Bake in preheated 350° oven for 40 minutes until cake tests done. Cool on rack. Frost with Pecan Butter Cream Icing. Makes 6 servings.

PECAN BUTTER CREAM ICING

1 egg yolk
½ cup butter or margarine, cut
   in ½-inch slices
2½ cups confectioners' sugar

1 teaspoon vanilla or 1
   tablespoon rum
½ cup chopped pecans (from
   previous recipe)

Fit processor with METAL BLADE. Add egg yolk and butter to processor bowl. Process 8 seconds. Add sugar and vanilla. Process 20 seconds, until smooth. Add pecans. Process 2 seconds. If weather is warm, mixture may be too soft to spread. Refrigerate until firm.

APPETIZERS

Spreads, Dips, Pantry-Shelf Quickies

ARTICHOKE SQUARES

An out-of-the-ordinary hors d'oeuvre that freezes well.

8 ounces sharp cheddar cheese,
  cut in 1-inch cubes
½ slice bread
2 6-ounce jars marinated
  artichoke hearts
1 small onion, quartered
1 clove garlic

2 tablespoons parsley, stems
  removed
4 eggs
½ teaspoon oregano
2–3 drops hot pepper sauce
Freshly ground pepper

Fit processor with METAL BLADE. Process cheese 5 seconds. Remove. Process bread 3 seconds. Remove. Drain artichokes, reserving marinade from one jar. Process onion and garlic for 3 seconds. Heat marinade in skillet and add onion and garlic. Sauté until soft. Process artichokes and parsley 5 seconds. Add eggs and seasonings. Process 2 seconds. Add onion mixture, crumbs and cheese. Process 3 seconds. Turn into 7 x 11-inch baking pan. Bake in preheated 350° oven for 30 minutes until set. Cool. Cut into small squares. Makes about 30 squares.

AVOCADO DIP

*Use as a dip for raw vegetables or a topping for
baked potatoes.*

2 medium ripe avocados
2 green onions, cut in ½-inch
    lengths
½ medium cucumber, peeled,
    seeded and cut in ½-inch
    lengths

1 clove garlic, sliced
Salt to taste
Freshly ground pepper
1 tablespoon vinegar

Fit processor with METAL BLADE. Peel avocados and cut into chunks. Process 10 seconds, until smooth. Add remaining ingredients and process 10 seconds. Turn into bowl and cover tightly. Chill. Makes about 1½ cups.

BABA GHANOUGH

This is a Middle Eastern "dip" with an exotic flavor.

2 medium eggplants
3 large cloves garlic
½ cup Tahini (sesame paste)

¼ cup water
⅓ cup lemon juice
Salt to taste

Place eggplants in baking pan. Bake in 400° oven for 45 minutes, or until very soft. Cool slightly and peel off skin. Fit processor with METAL BLADE. Remove eggplant flesh to processor. Add garlic cloves. Process 6 seconds, until smooth. Through feed tube add Tahini, water and lemon juice. Process 4 seconds. Add salt. Process 2 seconds. Mixture should be very smooth and light. Serve with a loaf of crusty dark bread. Makes about 3 cups.

CRISPY CHEESE SHAPES

*By using decorative cutters, these can make an
interesting snack to accompany soup, salad or drinks.*

8 ounces sharp cheddar cheese,
   cut in 1-inch cubes
4 ounces butter or margarine,
   cut in ½-inch slices
2 cups flour
½ teaspoon baking powder

1 teaspoon paprika
½ teaspoon salt
½ teaspoon prepared mustard
1 egg yolk
1 tablespoon sherry

Fit processor with METAL BLADE. Process cheese 5 seconds. Add butter. Process 2 seconds. Add remaining ingredients. Process 15 seconds, until well mixed. Turn out and wrap in waxed paper. Chill 1 hour or longer. Roll out on floured board. Cut in shapes. Place on lightly greased baking sheet. Bake in 400° oven for 10 to 12 minutes. These "shapes" may be frozen. Makes about 5 dozen.

CUCUMBER WALNUT DIP

*This is good served with whole wheat crackers or
pita bread.*

½ medium cucumber, peeled,
   seeded and diced
½ cup walnuts

1 clove garlic
1 tablespoon oil
1 cup sour cream

Fit processor with METAL BLADE. Process cucumber 3 seconds. Remove to bowl. Add walnuts, garlic and oil. Process 4 seconds. Add sour cream. Process 3 seconds. Combine with cucumber. Chill. Makes approximately 2 cups.

DELHI DIP

*A somewhat different hors d'oeuvre that always
wins compliments.*

8 ounces cooked chicken, cut in
   1-inch cubes (1 1-pound
   breast)
8 ounces cream cheese, cut in
   1-inch cubes

2 tablespoons chutney (see
   recipe for substitute)
1 teaspoon curry powder
¼ cup mayonnaise
¼ cup toasted slivered almonds

Fit processor with METAL BLADE. Process chicken 2 seconds. Fit processor with PLASTIC BLADE. Add cream cheese, chutney, curry powder and mayonnaise. Process 5 seconds, until well blended. Turn out into small baking or au gratin dish. Bake in 350° oven for 15 minutes. Sprinkle with almonds. Serve with sturdy chips for dipping. This mixture freezes well. If you do not have chutney, substitute 2 tablespoons orange marmalade, ½ teaspoon ground ginger and 2 teaspoons grated lemon rind. Makes 2 cups.

GUACAMOLE

*A wonderful, spicy Mexican mixture that can be used
as a dip, on sandwiches, as a base for fried eggs or as
a salad with chili.*

1 small onion, quartered
2 tablespoons parsley, stems
   removed
1 1-pound can green chili
   pepper
1 tomato, peeled and quartered

2 ripe avocados, peeled and cut
   into chunks
2 tablespoons lime juice
2 tablespoons oil
Salt to taste
Freshly ground pepper

Fit processor with METAL BLADE. Process onion and parsley for 3 seconds. Add chili pepper, tomato, avocados, lime juice and oil. Process 5 seconds. Season. Serve at room temperature with corn chips. Makes approximately 2 cups.

HOT MEXICAN DIP

Serve to a crowd.

½ pound Parmesan or Romano
   cheese, cut in 1-inch chunks
½ pound Jarlsberg cheese, cut in
   1-inch pieces

1 large onion
4 ounces green chilis
1 cup mayonnaise
1 cup sour cream

Fit processor with SHREDDING DISC. Grate Parmesan cheese. Remove to 2-quart casserole. Grate Jarlsberg and add to casserole. Fit processor with METAL BLADE. Process onion and chilis 10 seconds. Stir into cheeses with mayonnaise and sour cream, mixing well. Bake in preheated 350° oven for 30 minutes, until hot and puffy. Serve with corn chips or bread sticks. Makes about 6 cups.

MUSHROOM ROLLS

Pastry:
1¼ cups flour
½ cup butter or margarine, cut
   in ½-inch slices
½ teaspoon salt

3 tablespoons buttermilk or
   sour cream
1 egg yolk

Fit processor with METAL BLADE. Combine all ingredients and process for 30 seconds, until pastry forms a ball around spindle. Do not overprocess. Remove, wrap and chill.

Filling:
2 medium onions, quartered
1 12-ounce package fresh
   mushrooms, quartered
4 tablespoons butter or
   margarine

2 hardcooked eggs
Salt to taste
Freshly ground pepper
Prepared mustard

Fit processor with METAL BLADE. Heat butter in large skillet. Process half of onions and mushrooms together by pulsing 3 to 4 times until finely chopped. Turn into skillet, removing any large pieces. Return these to processor with remaining onions and mushrooms and process. Sauté mixture until onions are tender and mushrooms have given up their moisture. Meanwhile, with METAL BLADE, process eggs for 2 seconds. Add eggs and seasonings to mushroom mixture. Cool. Divide pastry into three pieces. Roll out on floured board as thin as possible without tearing. Brush with prepared mustard. Spread with mushroom mixture. Place rolls on lightly oiled baking sheet. Bake for 15 minutes in preheated 400° oven, until browned. Cut in ½-inch pieces and serve hot. Makes 3 dozen.

BAKED MUSHROOMS WITH HERBED SPINACH

*These mushrooms make a nice appetizer or
vegetable accompaniment.*

12 mushrooms, 2 inches in
   diameter
1 10-ounce package frozen leaf
   spinach
¼ cup parsley, stems removed
1 large green onion, sliced
1 stalk celery, cut in 1-inch
   lengths

2 tablespoons butter or
   margarine
1 tablespoon oil
½ teaspoon ground nutmeg
Salt to taste
Freshly ground pepper
1 or 2 slices bacon

Remove stems from mushrooms. Cook spinach. Strain, squeezing out excess liquid. Fit processor with METAL BLADE. Add mushroom stems, parsley, green onion and celery to processor. Process 2 seconds, until finely chopped. Heat butter and oil in skillet. Sauté mushroom mixture until soft, about 5 minutes. Process spinach 3 seconds. Add to skillet. Simmer all together for 5 minutes. Season. Stuff mushroom caps. Arrange on greased baking sheet. Place a 1-inch square piece of bacon on each mushroom. Bake in a 350° oven for 20 minutes, until bacon is crisp. Makes 4 servings.

BEEF LIVER PÂTÉ

Serve with thin slices of French bread or on a bed of lettuce with tomato slices and crackers.

2½ large onions
¼ cup water
5 tablespoons butter or
   margarine, divided

½ pound beef liver, cut in
   1-inch pieces
5 hardcooked eggs, quartered
1 teaspoon salt
¼ teaspoon freshly ground
   pepper

Fit processor with SLICING DISC. Slice 2 onions. Remove to saucepan with ¼ cup water. Bring to boil. Reduce heat; cover and simmer 7 to 10 minutes, or until all water cooks off. Add 3 tablespoons butter; cook until onions are lightly browned. Add liver. Cook, stirring, just until liver is cooked through. Cool slightly. Fit processor with METAL BLADE. Process remaining ½ onion for 3 seconds. Add liver mixture. Process 5 to 6 seconds. Add eggs. Process 5 seconds. Add remaining butter, salt and pepper. Process 4 seconds, until mixture is smooth and butter is incorporated. Refrigerate to cool completely. Makes 4 servings.

CARROT WALNUT PÂTÉ

A new and tasty combination of flavors.

4 medium carrots, scraped
1 cup walnuts
2 tablespoons oil
1 small onion, sliced
1 small clove garlic, sliced

Salt to taste
Freshly ground pepper
½ teaspoon nutmeg
1 tablespoon brandy

Fit processor with SLICING DISC. Slice carrots. Remove to saucepan. Cover with salted water and bring to a boil. Cover and cook until very tender. Meanwhile, fit processor with METAL BLADE. Process ¼ cup walnuts 3 seconds. Remove. Combine remaining walnuts and oil and process 10 seconds, until smooth. Add onion and garlic. Process 7 seconds. Add cooked, drained carrots, salt, pepper, nutmeg and brandy. Process 10 seconds, until mixture is very smooth. Turn out into bowl. Stir in chopped walnuts. Serve at room temperature with crackers or melba toast. Makes about 2 cups.

PANTRY SHELF PÂTÉS

*Keep the ingredients handy for
elegant emergency entertaining.*

PÂTÉ I

13-ounce can madrilene
2 hardcooked eggs, 1 sliced
4 slices pimento-stuffed green
olive
2 tablespoons walnuts

4-ounce can deviled ham spread
1 teaspoon prepared mustard
1 tablespoon sherry
½ teaspoon ground ginger
Freshly ground pepper

Pour enough madrilene into a flat-bottomed 1½-cup dish to cover the bottom to depth of ¼ inch. Place one slice of egg in the center. Arrange olive slices around egg. Place dish in freezer for 15 minutes until set. Fit processor with METAL BLADE. Process walnuts 2 seconds. Add ⅓ cup madrilene and remaining ingredients. Process 20 seconds, until smooth. Spread mixture over firm aspic. Chill until firm. Pour some of remaining madrilene over pâté just to cover. Chill until firm. Unmold onto plate and serve with crackers. Makes 4 to 6 servings.

PÂTÉ II

10-ounce can beef consommé
(with gelatin)
2 hardcooked eggs
2 tablespoons parsley, stems
removed
½-inch slice onion

4-ounce can liver spread
4-ounce can chicken spread
2 tablespoons brandy
½ teaspoon ground cumin
Freshly ground pepper

Pour enough consommé into 1-quart flat-bottomed dish to cover bottom to depth of ¼ inch. Slice one egg and arrange 5 slices in pattern in consommé. Place in freezer 15 minutes, until firm. Fit processor with METAL BLADE. Process parsley 3 seconds. Add remaining ingredients and remaining consommé. Process 20 seconds, until smooth. Spread over firm aspic. Chill. Turn out. Slice and serve on lettuce, garnished with tomato wedges and accompanied by French bread. Makes 6 to 8 servings.

SMOKED FISH PÂTÉ

A wonderful dish for a buffet.

1 envelope unflavored gelatin
¼ cup water
1 tablespoon butter or
    margarine
1 tablespoon flour
½ cup milk

¼ cup parsley, stems removed
2 3½-ounce cans smoked
    herring, drained
3 hardcooked eggs
½ cup mayonnaise
Freshly ground pepper

Soak gelatin in water. Heat butter in saucepan. Add flour and cook until bubbly. Add milk and cook, stirring, until thick and smooth. Stir in gelatin mixture until well blended. Remove from heat. Fit processor with METAL BLADE. Process parsley 8 seconds. Remove. Process smoked fish 3 seconds. Add 2 eggs. Process 2 seconds. Add mayonnaise, pepper and gelatin mixture. Process 4 seconds, until smooth. Turn into small mold or dish and chill overnight. Turn out. Fit processor with SLICING DISC. Slice remaining egg. Decorate top of pâté with sliced egg on a bed of chopped parsley. Accompany with crackers or melba toast. Makes 2 cups.

WATERCRESS CANAPÉ

Mixture can be made ahead and frozen.

1 jar (2½ ounces) dried beef
1 bunch watercress
    (approximately 6 ounces)
1 small onion, halved

1 package (3 ounces) cream
    cheese
Salt to taste
Freshly ground pepper

Remove dried beef from jar and cut crosswise into ½-inch slices. Cut stems off watercress and reserve for another use. (Good in soup and salad, finely chopped.) Fit processor with METAL BLADE. Process beef, watercress and onion for 10 seconds. Add cream cheese and process 10 seconds. Season. Process 1 second. Refrigerate overnight. Spread on whole wheat bread for sandwiches. Makes about 2 cups.

SOUPS

Creamy, Chunky, Whole-Meal

BASQUE SOUP GRATINÉE

*This winter squash soup makes a filling main course
for a "soup supper."*

1 2½-pound Buttercup squash
  (or any golden winter squash)
1 slice whole wheat bread
2 tablespoons butter or
  margarine
1 tablespoon oil

1 large onion, quartered
4 cups chicken bouillon
Salt to taste
Freshly ground pepper
6 ounces Gruyere or Swiss
  cheese, in one piece

Cut squash in large pieces. Steam over boiling water until very tender. Fit processor with METAL BLADE. Process bread 10 seconds. Turn out onto baking sheet and toast crumbs in preheated 350° oven for 10 minutes. Heat butter and oil in skillet. Process onion 5 seconds. Sauté onion in skillet until soft. When squash is cooked, scrape flesh from skin, discarding seeds and strings. Process squash with onion, crumbs and 2 cups bouillon 20 seconds, until smooth. This may have to be done in 2 batches. Turn into saucepan and add remaining bouillon. Season. Fit processor with SLICING DISC. Slice cheese. Heat soup and pour into ovenproof bowls. Spread cheese slices over top of soup. They will sink slightly. Put bowls on baking sheet. Heat in preheated 450° oven for 10 minutes, until cheese is melted. Serve with cranberry cornbread, green salad and apple crumb pie. Makes 4 servings.

CAULIFLOWER AND SHRIMP SOUP

*If you bought the biggest head of cauliflower
and have a lot left over, here is a delicious main
dish you can make.*

3 cups cooked cauliflower
2 cups chicken bouillon
1 4½-ounce can tiny shrimp,
   drained
2 cups milk

¼ teaspoon mace
Salt to taste
Freshly ground pepper
¼ cup slivered toasted almonds
   (optional)

Fit processor with METAL BLADE. Process cauliflower and bouillon for 20 seconds or until smooth. (It may take a bit longer.) Add half of shrimp and process 5 seconds more. Turn into saucepan and add milk and seasonings. Heat to boiling point. Serve in bowls, with remaining shrimp and almonds sprinkled over top. A marinated vegetable salad and corn muffins are a good accompaniment. Makes 4 servings.

CELERY SENEGALESE

A refreshing soup to be served hot or cold.

4 medium stalks celery, cut in
   1-inch lengths
3 tablespoons butter or
   margarine
1 medium onion, quartered
1 tablespoon flour

1–2 teaspoons curry powder
4 cups chicken bouillon
Freshly ground pepper
¼ cup heavy cream
Salt to taste
Paprika

Fit processor with METAL BLADE. Process celery 4 seconds. Turn into saucepan with butter. Process onion for 3 seconds. Add to saucepan. Sauté vegetables for 3 minutes, stirring. Cover pan and simmer for 7 to 8 minutes, until soft. Sprinkle flour and curry powder over vegetables and cook for 2 minutes. Add bouillon and bring to a boil. Reduce heat and simmer until celery is very tender. Process until mixture is smooth, about 15 seconds. Before serving, whip cream until stiff and add salt and paprika. Put a spoonful of cream on each serving. Makes 6 servings.

CREAMY MUSHROOM SOUP

Just the thing to start a winter dinner.

½ pound mushrooms, quartered
3 tablespoons butter or
  margarine
2 stalks celery, cut in ½-inch
  pieces

2 medium green onions or 1
  small onion, sliced
4 cups chicken bouillon
½ cup cream
Salt to taste
Freshly ground pepper

Fit processor with METAL BLADE. Process half the mushrooms for 3 minutes. Heat butter in saucepan and add mushrooms. Process remaining mushrooms for 3 minutes. Add to saucepan. Process celery 3 seconds. Remove ¼ cup chopped celery and set aside. Add remaining celery to saucepan. Process green onions 2 minutes. Add to saucepan. Sauté vegetables for 2 to 3 minutes. Add bouillon and bring to a boil. Reduce heat to medium. Cover pan and simmer for 20 minutes. Return to processor and process 10 seconds. This may have to be done in two or more batches. Return to saucepan. Season with salt and pepper. Add cream and reheat but do not boil. Sprinkle each serving with chopped celery. Makes 4 servings.

CURRIED CARROT BISQUE

1 pound carrots, scraped
¼ cup butter or margarine
2 medium onions, peeled and
  quartered
2 medium apples, peeled, cored
  and quartered
1 tablespoon packed brown
  sugar

1 teaspoon curry powder, or to
  taste
6 cups chicken bouillon
1 cup milk or light cream
Salt to taste
Freshly ground pepper
2 tablespoons chopped parsley
  (optional)

Cut carrots into chunks and place in saucepan. Cover with salted water. Boil until tender. Heat butter in skillet. Fit processor with METAL BLADE. Pulse onions 3 to 4 times, chopping coarsely. Turn into skillet. Add apples to processor. Pulse 2 to 3 times. Add to skillet. Sauté mixture until tender. Stir in sugar and curry powder. Cook 2 minutes longer. Drain carrots. Process carrots and onion mixture until smooth. Turn into saucepan; add bouillon. Bring to a boil. Reduce heat and simmer 15 minutes. Add milk and seasoning. Serve hot with parsley garnish or chill and serve with chopped raw apple garnish. Makes 6 servings.

CURRIED CLAM AND CELERY BISQUE

Serve with a salad on a hot summer day.

2 medium stalks celery with
    leaves, cut in 1-inch lengths
2 8-ounce cans minced clams,
    with juice

2 cups half-and-half
1 teaspoon curry powder
Salt to taste

Fit processor with METAL BLADE. Process celery 10 seconds. Add clams. Process 10 seconds. Add half-and-half, curry powder and salt. Process 20 seconds, until smooth. Chill. This may have to be done in 2 batches. Makes 4 servings.

GARDEN VEGETABLE SOUP

Combining the best from the garden.

2 tablespoons margarine
1 medium onion, quartered
1 small green pepper, seeded,
    cut in 1-inch pieces
1 clove garlic
2 large tomatoes, peeled and
    quartered
2 medium carrots, scrubbed

1 small zucchini
3 cups beef bouillon
¼ pound green beans, cut in
    1-inch pieces (about 1 cup)
½ teaspoon basil
½ teaspoon pepper
2 tablespoons cornstarch
¼ cup water

Fit processor with METAL BLADE. Put margarine in large saucepan over medium heat. Process onion 4 seconds, until chopped. Add to saucepan. Process pepper and garlic 3 seconds. Add to onion. Cook, stirring frequently, 3 to 4 minutes. Process tomatoes 3 seconds. Fit processor with SLICING DISC. Slice carrots and zucchini. Add bouillon, tomatoes, carrots, beans, zucchini, basil and pepper to saucepan. Bring to boil. Reduce heat, cover and simmer 15 minutes, or until vegetables are tender. Mix cornstarch with water until smooth; add to soup. Stirring, bring to boil; boil 1 minute. Serve hot. Makes 4 servings.

SPRING PEA SOUP

1 small head iceberg or romaine lettuce	3 cups chicken bouillon
1 green onion, white part only	1 cup milk
2 tablespoons butter or margarine	Salt
1 pound fresh peas or 1 10-ounce package frozen peas	Freshly ground pepper
	1 teaspoon sugar
	2 tablespoons mint leaves

Fit processor with SLICING DISC. Wash lettuce and green onion and dry. Slice both vegetables. Heat butter in saucepan. Sauté lettuce and leek for 2 minutes. Add peas. Cook for 2 minutes. Add bouillon. Bring to a boil. Reduce heat and simmer, covered, for 20 minutes. Fit processor with METAL BLADE. Process soup 20 seconds. This will have to be done in at least 2 batches. Return to saucepan and add milk, salt, pepper and sugar. Heat. Process mint leaves for 3 seconds. Sprinkle over soup. Makes 4 servings.

VICHYSSOISE

Be sure to serve this classic soup icy cold.

4 medium all-purpose potatoes, peeled and cut into chunks	5 cups chicken bouillon
2 green onions, white part only, cut in 1-inch lengths	1 cup heavy cream
1 medium onion, quartered	Salt to taste
4 tablespoons butter or margarine	Freshly ground pepper
	½ teaspoon nutmeg
	Chopped chives for garnish

Fit processor with METAL BLADE. Process potatoes 3 seconds. Remove. Process green and regular onions 4 seconds. Heat butter in heavy saucepan. Add potato-and-onion mixture. Sauté for 3 minutes. Add bouillon. Bring to a boil. Cover pan and simmer for 30 minutes. Return to processor in 2 batches. Process 30 seconds, until very smooth. Turn into large bowl or pitcher. Stir in cream and seasonings. Serve sprinkled with chives. Makes 6 servings.

WELSH RABBIT AND KIELBASA SOUP

Partially freezing the sausage makes it easier to slice.

2 ounces cheddar cheese
½ pound kielbasa, frozen until
   firm but not solid
2 cans (11 ounces each)
   condensed cheddar-cheese
   soup

2 teaspoons prepared mustard
1 soup can water
1 cup beer
¼ teaspoon freshly ground
   pepper

Fit processor with SHREDDING DISC. Shred cheese. Remove. Fit processor with serrated SLICING DISC. Slice kielbasa into rounds. Remove. In large saucepan, combine soup and mustard until blended. Add water, beer and pepper. Bring to boil. Add kielbasa, lower heat and simmer 10 minutes. Before serving, sprinkle with cheddar. Makes 4 servings.

GARLIC SOUP

Hearty meal-in-one soup with salad and dessert.

3 tablespoons parsley, stems
   removed
1 ounce Parmesan cheese, cut
   in ½-inch cubes
1 medium onion, quartered
4 cloves garlic, split

¼ cup oil
4 slices French or Italian bread,
   ½ inch thick
6 cups chicken broth
Freshly ground pepper to taste
4 eggs

Fit processor with METAL BLADE. Process parsley 5 seconds. Remove. Process cheese 7 to 8 seconds. Remove. Pulse onion 4 or 5 times, until chopped. Sauté garlic in hot oil in large saucepan until lightly browned; discard garlic. Brush one side of bread with half the oil; arrange on cookie sheet, oil side up. Bake in preheated 350° oven 15 to 18 minutes, or until well toasted; set aside. Sauté onion in remaining oil until tender. Add broth and pepper; bring to boil; reduce heat and simmer. Break eggs one at a time into cup and slip into broth. Poach 3 minutes or to desired doneness. Meanwhile, place toasted bread in tureen or individual soup bowls. Top each slice with an egg and fill tureen with broth. Sprinkle with Parmesan and parsley. Serve at once. Makes 4 servings.

SCOTCH BROTH

Serve with honey-buttered scones and oatmeal apple crisp.

2 pounds lamb bones
1 pound boneless lamb, cut in
   1-inch cubes
2 quarts water
1½ teaspoons salt
¼ teaspoon pepper
1 bay leaf
2 large potatoes, peeled
4 medium carrots

2 green onions
1 large onion, quartered
4 ribs celery
1 10-ounce package frozen lima
   beans
½ cup pearl barley
1 teaspoon thyme
2 tablespoons chopped parsley

In kettle or Dutch oven bring bones, lamb, water, salt, pepper and bay leaf to boil. Remove scum. Reduce heat, cover and simmer 1 to 1½ hours. Fit processor with SLICING DISC. Slice potatoes and put into bowl of cold water. Place carrots in feed tube horizontally and slice. Remove. Place green onions in feed tube horizontally and slice. Remove. Fit processor with METAL BLADE. Pulse onion 4 to 5 times, until coarsely chopped. Remove and discard lamb bones from soup. Skim off fat. Stir in vegetables and remaining ingredients except parsley. Return to boil. Reduce heat; simmer, covered, about 45 minutes, or until lamb and vegetables are tender. Discard bay leaf. Sprinkle with parsley. Makes 6 servings.

SPLIT PEA SOUP

2 large celery ribs
2 large carrots
1 pound split green peas
2 ham hocks (about 1½ pounds)
1 medium onion studded with 3
   cloves

1 bay leaf
1 teaspoon salt
½ teaspoon freshly ground
   pepper
7 cups water

Fit processor with SLICING DISC. Slice celery. Remove to kettle or Dutch oven. Slice carrots. Add to celery with remaining ingredients. Bring to boil. Reduce heat, cover and simmer 2½ hours, or until ham is very tender and peas are very soft. Remove ham hocks, onion and bay leaf; discard onion and bay leaf. Cut meat from hocks. Fit processor with METAL BLADE. Process soup 10 seconds until puréed. This must be done in 3 or 4 batches. Return meat to soup. Adjust seasonings. Makes 8 servings.

MAIN DISHES

Pâtés, Loaves, Roulades, Stews

APPLE CHEESE SOUFFLÉ

Apples and cheese have always been a winning combination in any form.

½ pound cheddar cheese
3 tablespoons butter or
   margarine
3 tablespoons flour
½ cup cider
½ cup milk
1 teaspoon prepared mustard

Salt to taste
Freshly ground pepper
5 egg yolks
1 medium tart apple, cored
   and quartered
6 egg whites

Fit processor with SHREDDING DISC. Shred cheese. Remove. Combine butter and flour in saucepan and cook over medium-high heat, stirring, until smooth and bubbling. Add cider and milk and cook, stirring, until thick and smooth. Add mustard and seasonings. Stir in yolks one at a time. Stir in cheese. Butter a 2-quart soufflé dish. Fit processor with SLICING DISC. Place apple in feed tube, cut side down, and slice. Beat egg whites until stiff and fold into yolk mixture. Turn half of soufflé mixture into dish. Cover with apple slices. Fill dish with remaining soufflé mixture. Bake at 350° for 40 to 45 minutes, until golden and firm. Serve immediately. Makes 5 servings.

BEEF-PORK LOAF

¾ cup cornflakes
1 large rib celery, cut in 1-inch
  pieces
1 medium onion, sliced
1½ pounds round steak, well
  trimmed

1 medium carrot
½ pound pork sausage
  meat
2 eggs
1½ teaspoons salt
½ teaspoon freshly ground
  pepper

Fit processor with METAL BLADE. Process cornflakes 7 seconds. Remove to large bowl. Process celery 5 seconds. Remove to bowl. Process onion 5 seconds. Remove to bowl. Process beef, ½ pound at a time, 5 seconds. Remove to bowl. Fit processor with SHREDDING DISC. Shred carrot. Remove to bowl. Add remaining ingredients to bowl and mix all together until well blended. In shallow baking dish, shape mixture into 8 x 4-inch loaf. Bake in preheated 350° oven 1 hour. Let stand 5 to 10 minutes. Makes 8 servings. The loaf can be frozen for 2 to 3 weeks.

CHINESE-STYLE BEEF, ONION AND ZUCCHINI

*Doing all the slicing ahead means very little to do just
before dinner.*

1 pound round steak, about ½
  inch thick
½ cup chicken bouillon
2 tablespoons soy sauce
1 tablespoon each cornstarch,
  catsup and dry sherry

½ teaspoon ground ginger
1 large zucchini, about ½ pound
1 large onion
3 tablespoons oil, divided

Cut steak in pieces so it can lie in feed tube horizontally. Freeze 30 to 40 minutes, until firm. Combine bouillon, soy sauce, cornstarch, catsup, sherry and ginger in small bowl. Set aside. Fit processor with SLICING DISC. Cut meat strips into thin crosswise slices. Remove. Cut zucchini into 2½-inch-long pieces to fit in feed tube horizontally. Slice. Remove. Slice onion. Remove. In large skillet, heat 2 tablespoons oil until very hot but not smoking. Add onion and zucchini. Stir fry over medium heat 3 to 5 minutes, or until almost crisp-tender. Remove with slotted spoon. Heat remaining 1 tablespoon oil until very hot but not smoking. Add steak. Stir fry until it loses its pink color. Stir in vegetable mixture. Add cornstarch mixture and stir until sauce has thickened. Serve immediately, with hot rice tossed with bean sprouts. Makes 4 servings.

BOILED PORK DINNER

The meat can be served hot with vegetables or cold with Cranberry Catsup.

1 smoked pork shoulder
   roll (3 pounds)
Water
4 medium carrots

4 medium turnips, peeled
   (about 1¼ pounds)
1 pound cabbage, cut in 4
   wedges
Cranberry Catsup (recipe on
   page 145)

In Dutch oven or large heavy saucepot, bring pork and enough water to cover to boil. Reduce heat; cover and simmer 45 minutes. Fit processor with SLICING DISC. Slice carrots. Remove to pot with meat. Slice turnips. Add to pot. Cook, covered, 25 to 30 minutes, or until vegetables are almost fork tender. Add cabbage; cook 15 minutes, or until vegetables and pork are tender. Serve half the meat hot, sliced thin, with the vegetables. Refrigerate remaining meat. Slice thin before serving cold with Cranberry Catsup. Makes 8 servings.

DANISH MEATBALLS

These can be made any size, for any occasion. They freeze well.

½ cup parsley, stems removed
1 medium onion, quartered
1 pound lean beef, well
   trimmed, cut in ½-inch cubes
1 pound pork, well trimmed
1 egg
¼ cup sour cream
½ cup rolled oats
1 teaspoon prepared mustard
Salt to taste
Freshly ground pepper

2 tablespoons shortening
1 green onion, sliced
¼ pound mushrooms, quartered
3 tablespoons butter or
   margarine
3 tablespoons flour
1 cup beef bouillon
½ cup milk
¼ cup white wine
¼ teaspoon ground nutmeg
¼ teaspoon ground allspice

Fit processor with METAL BLADE. Process parsley for 5 seconds. Remove half and set aside. Add onion and process 3 seconds. Remove mixture to large bowl. Process meat ½ pound at a time. Pulse 3 to 4 times, until meat is finely ground. Remove to bowl. Add egg, sour cream, oats and mustard to processor. Process 3 seconds. Add to bowl. Mix well with hands, adding salt and pepper. Shape into walnut-sized balls. Heat shortening in large skillet. Brown meatballs on all sides. Slice onion. Quarter mushrooms. Process together for 3 seconds, or until finely chopped. Heat butter in large skillet. Sauté mushroom mixture for 5 minutes. Sprinkle with flour. Cook for 2 minutes. Add bouillon and milk. Cook until thick and smooth. Add wine and cook for 5 minutes. Add seasonings. Turn meatballs into ovenproof 1½-quart baking dish. Cover with mushroom sauce. Bake in preheated 350° oven for 30 minutes. Sprinkle with remaining parsley. Serve with steamed new potatoes. Makes 6 servings.

BELGIAN BEER STEW

A nice winter dish that tastes better if made ahead.
Serve beer or ale with it.

1½ pounds top or bottom round	1 tablespoon oil
Salt and pepper	2 tablespoons brown sugar,
1 12-ounce can beer	packed
3 large onions	1 teaspoon prepared mustard
2 tablespoons butter or	1 tablespoon flour
margarine	¼ cup parsley, stems removed

Trim all fat off meat. Cut meat in pieces so they fit feed tube when placed horizontally. Wrap meat in plastic wrap and place in coldest part of freezer. Freeze for 40 minutes, or until firm. Fit processor with SLICING DISC. Put meat into feed tube and, with gentle pressure, slice it. Turn meat into baking dish. Sprinkle with salt and pepper. Add ¼ cup beer. Cover dish and place in preheated 325° oven. Bake for 45 minutes. Meanwhile, slice onions in processor. Heat butter and oil in large skillet. Sauté onions over medium heat until golden and soft. Stir in sugar and mustard. Sprinkle flour over onions; cook for 2 minutes. Add remaining beer; cook for 2 minutes. Stir onion mixture into beef. Bake, covered, for 1½ hours, until meat is very tender. Fit processor with METAL BLADE. Process parsley for 3 seconds. Sprinkle over stew. Serve with noodles and coleslaw. Makes 4 or 5 servings.

STUFFED CABBAGE JAMBALAYA

1 medium head Savoy cabbage
1 medium stalk celery, cut in 1-inch pieces
2 medium onions, quartered
½ medium green pepper, seeded, cut in 1-inch pieces
2 tablespoons bacon fat or oil
½ pound smoked ham, cut in 1-inch cubes
1 cup cooked chicken, diced
2 tablespoons parsley, stems removed
1 teaspoon chili powder, or to taste
Salt to taste
Freshly ground pepper
1 cup cooked rice
2 cups canned plum tomatoes, chopped and drained

Cut core out of cabbage and remove leaves carefully. Drop leaves into large pot of boiling salted water. Blanch 3 to 4 minutes, until just limp. Drain and dry. Remove large end of center vein on each leaf. Fit processor with METAL BLADE. Process celery 3 seconds. Remove to bowl. Process onions 3 to 4 seconds. Remove to bowl. Process green pepper 3 seconds. Remove to bowl. Heat fat in large skillet. Add chopped vegetables and sauté until just tender. Process ham 3 to 4 seconds. Add to skillet. Process chicken 2 seconds. Add to skillet. Process parsley 3 seconds. Add to skillet seasonings, rice and parsley. Simmer 3 minutes. Remove from heat. Place spoonfuls of mixture on cabbage leaves and roll up, tucking in sides. Place rolls seam side down in greased shallow 2-quart baking dish. Pour tomatoes over and around rolls. Cover and bake 1 hour in preheated 350° oven. To serve: Drain off excess liquid and spread tomatoes over rolls. Accompany with parslied potatoes or noodles. Makes 10 rolls.

CHICKEN BREASTS AUX POIRES

A nice dish combining fruit and cheese with chicken.

2 whole chicken breasts, (approximately 1 pound each), split, skinned and trimmed of excess fat
Salt to taste
Freshly ground pepper
3 tablespoons butter or margarine
1 tablespoon oil
3 medium ripe, firm pears
4 ounces ripe Brie cheese
¼-inch slice onion
1 cup dry Vermouth
½ cup cream

Sprinkle chicken breasts on all sides with salt and pepper. Heat 2 tablespoons butter and oil in large skillet. Sauté breasts on both sides until browned. Meanwhile, fit processor with METAL BLADE. Peel and core 2 pears. Process for 2 seconds. Add to skillet. Cut Brie into chunks and process with onion for 3 seconds. Add to skillet. Add Vermouth to skillet. Cover and cook over medium heat for 20 minutes. Remove chicken breasts to serving dish. Slice remaining pear, leaving skin on. Add remaining 1 tablespoon butter to skillet. Sauté pear slices for 5 minutes, until glazed. Arrange in overlapping slices beside chicken breasts. Process contents of skillet for 7 seconds, until smooth. Add cream and process for 2 seconds. Return to skillet and bring to a boil. Pour over chicken breasts. Serve immediately. This may be made ahead and reheated in 325° oven. Serve with parslied rice and green beans. Makes 4 servings.

BAKED STUFFED BROILERS

2 tablespoons lemon juice	3 slices bread
1 clove garlic, mashed	6 tablespoons pecans
½ cup white wine or Vermouth	½ large unpeeled navel orange, quartered
½ cup oil	2 apples, cored and quartered
Salt to taste	2 onions, quartered
Freshly ground pepper	
3 2-pound broiler chickens, split	

Combine lemon juice, garlic, wine, oil, salt and pepper. Arrange chickens in one layer in large pan. Pour wine mixture over chickens. Cover and let stand overnight, turning occasionally. Fit processor with METAL BLADE. Process bread 10 seconds. Remove to large bowl. Process pecans 4 seconds. Add to bread. Process orange 15 seconds. Add to bread. Process apples 5 seconds. Add to bowl and toss all together. Fit processor with SLICING DISC. Slice onions. Pat chickens dry. Pack bread stuffing into cavities. Place chickens, stuffing side down, in baking pan. Arrange onion slices over top and sprinkle with salt and pepper. Pour marinade into bottom of pan. Bake in preheated 350° oven for 40 minutes, basting occasionally. Serve with sautéed apple rings and banana slices. Makes 6 servings.

CHICKEN WITH CUCUMBER-HORSERADISH SAUCE

Plain baked chicken takes on a new look with this unusual sauce.

3 pounds chicken pieces
1 teaspoon salt
2 teaspoons paprika
2 tablespoons lemon juice
1 medium cucumber, peeled, seeded and diced
2 tablespoons fresh horseradish root, or 2 teaspoons bottled horseradish

2 tablespoons butter or margarine
2 tablespoons flour
1 cup chicken bouillon
2 tablespoons sour cream
1 tablespoon snipped dill weed

Arrange chicken pieces in one layer on baking dish. Sprinkle with salt, paprika and lemon juice. Bake in preheated 350° oven for 20 minutes. Meanwhile, fit processor with METAL BLADE. Process cucumber 3 seconds, or until finely chopped. Add horseradish and process 2 seconds. Heat butter in saucepan and sauté cucumber mixture for 5 minutes. Stir in flour and cook 2 minutes. Add bouillon and cook until thickened. Stir in sour cream and dill. Pour over chicken and bake for additional 15 minutes. Serve with boiled potatoes and a green vegetable. Makes 6 servings.

CHICKEN LEGS CORDON BLEU

A variation on an old theme.

2 slices bread
4 ounces ham, cut in 1-inch pieces
4 ounces Swiss cheese, cut in 1-inch pieces

2 tablespoons butter or margarine
4 chicken legs (drumsticks and thighs)
2 tablespoons prepared mustard
1½ cups tomato sauce

Fit processor with METAL BLADE. Process bread 8 seconds, or until fine crumbs. Remove to shallow dish. Combine ham, cheese and butter in processor. Process 5 seconds, until well blended. Remove to bowl. With fingers, loosen the skin on the drumsticks and thighs and push ham mixture between skin and flesh. Pat skin back into place. Brush chicken pieces all over with a light coating of mustard. Roll in crumbs. Place in one layer in shallow baking dish. Bake in preheated 350° oven for 30 minutes. Pour tomato sauce over all and bake 10 minutes longer. Serve with sautéed mushrooms and buttered noodles. Makes 4 servings.

CREOLE CHICKEN

A slightly different chicken dish that appeals to all ages. Great for a buffet.

1 4-pound frying chicken	3 tablespoons oil
Salt to taste	2 cups canned plum tomatoes,
1 tablespoon lemon juice	chopped and drained
1 medium green pepper, seeded,	1 hardcooked egg
cut in 1-inch pieces	Hot pepper sauce
3 medium stalks celery, cut in	Freshly ground pepper
1-inch lengths	2 slices buttered bread
2 medium onions, quartered	

Cut chicken into 6 serving pieces. Place in one layer in baking dish. Sprinkle with salt and lemon juice. Cover tightly with foil. Bake in 425° oven for 30 to 35 minutes, until chicken is cooked. Cool, skin, and remove meat from bones. Dice in bite-size pieces. Fit processor with METAL BLADE. Process green pepper 4 seconds, until fairly fine. Process celery 5 seconds. Remove METAL BLADE and replace with SLICING DISC. Slice onions. Heat oil in large skillet. Turn vegetables into skillet. Sauté over medium heat for 10 minutes, stirring occasionally. Add tomatoes. Cook until mixture is fairly thick. Fit processor with METAL BLADE. Process egg for 2 seconds. Stir into vegetables. Season with hot pepper sauce, salt and pepper. Stir in diced chicken. Turn into greased 2-quart baking dish. Process buttered bread slices for 3 seconds. Sprinkle crumbs over chicken mixture. Bake in preheated 350° oven for 30 minutes. Serve with Mushroom Rice (see page 85 for recipe). Makes 6 servings.

GEORGIA BAKED CHICKEN

Peanut sauce? Believe it or not, it's delicious and not too rich.

1 3½–4 pound frying chicken, cut into serving pieces
2 tablespoons melted butter or margarine
1 tablespoon lemon juice
Salt to taste
1 teaspoon paprika

¾ cup roasted peanuts
¾ cup cream
3 tablespoons sherry
½-inch piece fresh ginger root, or 1 teaspoon ground ginger
1 teaspoon soy sauce

Place chicken pieces in one layer in baking dish. Sprinkle with butter and lemon juice. Season with salt and paprika. Bake in preheated 350° oven for 30 minutes. Meanwhile, fit processor with METAL BLADE. Place peanuts and cream in processor and process 10 seconds. Add sherry, ginger root and soy sauce. Process 5 seconds. Spread over chicken pieces. Bake 20 minutes longer. Serve with rice. Makes 4 servings.

ORANGE BLOSSOM CHICKEN

We use the whole orange (all but the seeds) for a very orange-y flavor in both stuffing and sauce.

½ navel orange, cut from top to bottom
1 slice bread
3 sprigs parsley
½-inch slice onion
½ teaspoon ginger
2 whole chicken breasts (1 pound each), split, skinned and boned

Salt to taste
Freshly ground pepper
½ cup orange juice
2 tablespoons lemon juice
¼ cup honey
½ teaspoon curry powder
1 teaspoon cornstarch dissolved in 1 tablespoon water

Fit processor with METAL BLADE. Remove white pith core of orange and cut into 4 pieces. Process 7 seconds, until finely chopped. Remove to small bowl. Add bread, parsley and onion and process 5 seconds, until finely grated. Add to orange. Add ginger and stir together. Place chicken breasts between sheets of waxed paper and pound until thin. Spread each breast with orange mixture. Sprinkle with salt and pepper. Roll up, tucking in sides. Place in greased baking dish in one layer. Combine orange juice, lemon juice, honey and curry powder in small saucepan. Heat, stirring, until blended. Pour over chicken. Cover dish with foil. Bake in 425° oven for 20 minutes, until chicken is firm to the touch and opaque. Remove to serving dish. Pour pan juices into saucepan. Heat, adding cornstarch mixture. Stir until thick. Pour over chicken. Cut remaining orange half into wedges and garnish chicken. Serve with rice mixed with raisins and chopped peanuts. Makes 4 servings.

ROAST CHICKEN WITH SPINACH SOUFFLÉ STUFFING

A scrumptious Sunday dinner.

1 lemon
2 slices firm white bread
1 cup ricotta cheese
1 whole egg
1 egg white
½ teaspoon ground nutmeg
Salt to taste

Freshly ground pepper
½ 10-ounce bag fresh spinach, stems removed
1 6–7 pound roasting chicken
3 tablespoons melted shortening
1 tablespoon lemon juice

Remove peel from half the lemon with vegetable peeler. Fit METAL BLADF into processor. Put bread into processor with lemon peel. Process 10 seconds. Add ricotta cheese, egg, egg white and seasonings. Process 5 seconds, until blended. Remove METAL BLADE. Insert SHREDDING DISC. Push spinach leaves through feed tube and shred. Turn mixture into bowl and toss together. Stuff cavity of chicken and close opening with skewer. Set chicken on its side on rack in roasting pan. Brush with shortening and lemon juice. Add ¼ inch water to bottom of pan. Place in preheated 400° oven and roast for 25 minutes, basting after 15 minutes. Turn chicken to other side and brush with shortening and lemon juice. Roast for 25 minutes. Turn breast side up, basting, and roast for 20 minutes. Let chicken rest 10 minutes before carving. Serve with glazed onions and chutney. Makes 6 servings.

ZUCCHINI-STUFFED CHICKEN BREASTS

We keep finding new uses for this versatile vegetable.

2 whole chicken breasts (1 pound each), split, skinned and boned
2 ounces Parmesan cheese, cut in 1-inch cubes
1 small zucchini, unpeeled, cut in ½-inch slices
½ medium onion, halved
2 tablespoons butter or margarine

½ cup uncooked rice
½ cup chicken bouillon
1 teaspoon poultry seasoning
Salt to taste
Freshly ground pepper
2 tablespoons brandy
½ cup dry Vermouth
¼ cup heavy cream
1 tablespoon cornstarch

Pound chicken breasts between sheets of waxed paper until thin. Fit processor with METAL BLADE. Process cheese for 5 seconds, until finely grated. Remove. Process zucchini 4 to 5 seconds. Process onion 3 seconds. Heat butter in skillet and add vegetables. Sauté 3 minutes. Add rice and sauté 2 minutes. Add bouillon. Cover and simmer 15 minutes, until liquid is absorbed and rice is almost tender. Stir in poultry seasoning, salt, pepper and half of cheese. Spread mixture on chicken breasts. Roll up, tucking in sides. Place breasts in one layer in baking dish. Add brandy and Vermouth to skillet and bring to boil. Pour over chicken. Cover. Bake in preheated 350° oven for 40 minutes. Remove chicken to serving platter. Pour liquid remaining in pan into saucepan and set over medium heat. Dissolve cornstarch in cream. Stir into liquid and cook until mixture is thickened and smooth. Pour over chicken. Sprinkle with remaining cheese. Place dish in oven until cheese is melted. Serve with sautéed mushroom slices and grilled tomatoes. This dish can be prepared ahead and reheated. Makes 4 servings.

CHILI CON CARNE

A true chili lover knows that the meat must be finely chopped, not ground. Here is where the processor proves especially worthwhile.

1½ pounds round steak or
   chuck
2 tablespoons oil
1 medium green pepper, seeded,
   cut in 1-inch pieces
1 medium onion
1 cup chopped tomatoes

1½ teaspoons ground cumin
   seed
1–2 teaspoons chili powder
2 cups water
Salt to taste
1 1-pound can kidney beans
1 cup tomato juice

Trim meat of all fat. Cut into 1-inch cubes. Fit processor with METAL BLADE. Process meat ½ pound at a time. Distribute cubes evenly around bowl. Pulse 4 to 5 times. Heat 1 tablespoon oil in large skillet. Sauté meat until all moisture has evaporated and meat begins to stick to pan. This will take 15 to 20 minutes. Process green pepper 3 seconds. Fit processor with SLICING DISC. Slice onion. Remove meat from skillet. Add remaining 1 tablespoon oil. Sauté pepper and onion for 5 minutes. Stir in tomatoes and spices. Simmer for 5 minutes. Add water and salt. Return meat to pan. Cover and cook over low heat for 1 hour. Drain and rinse beans. Add to meat with tomato juice. Cook for 1 hour longer. Serve over rice with guacamole and cornbread. Makes 6 servings.

CRUSTLESS MUSHROOM QUICHE

There's more than one way to eliminate a few calories.

20 small-size wheat crackers
2 tablespoons butter or
   margarine
1 large green onion or ½ small
   regular onion
¾ pound mushrooms

¼ cup sherry
Salt to taste
Freshly ground pepper
2 eggs
1 cup milk
½ teaspoon nutmeg

Fit processor with METAL BLADE. Process crackers for 10 seconds. Remove and spread over bottom of buttered 8-inch pie pan. Heat butter in skillet. Slice onion and process 3 seconds. Add to skillet. Fit processor with SLICING DISC. Stack mushrooms on sides in feed tube. Slice. Remove to skillet. Sauté for 3 minutes, stirring. Add sherry, salt and pepper. Simmer for 5 minutes. With slotted spoon, remove mushrooms to pie pan. Raise heat and reduce liquid in skillet to 2 tablespoons. Beat together the eggs, milk, nutmeg and reduced liquid. Pour over mushrooms. Bake in preheated 350° oven for 30 minutes. Let stand for 10 minutes before serving. This can be frozen. Makes 6 servings.

DUCK PÂTÉ

*A wonderful holiday dish that makes one duck
go a long way.*

1 4½–5 pound duckling	½ pound pork fat
½ cup Madeira wine	Rind of ½ orange, cut in strips
¼ cup walnuts	½ teaspoon thyme
8 dried apricots or peaches, quartered	2 tablespoons brandy
3 dried pears, quartered	2 eggs
½ pound ham, cut in ½-inch cubes	Salt to taste
½ pound pork, cut in ½-inch cubes	Freshly ground pepper
	½ pound fatty bacon
	2 bay leaves

Skin duckling. Cut off all fat and remove breasts in one piece. Place breasts in dish and cover with Madeira. Let stand overnight. Cut all remaining meat off duck carcass. Fit processor with METAL BLADE. Process nuts and dried fruits together 15 seconds. Remove. Add duck meat, except breasts, to processor. Process 10 seconds, until smooth. Remove to bowl. Process ham 10 seconds. Add to duck. Process pork and pork fat 10 seconds. Add to duck. Combine orange rind, thyme, brandy, eggs, salt and pepper and process 10 seconds. Add to duck. Mix well with hands, blending until smooth. Line a 2-quart terrine or loaf pan with bacon slices, saving some for later. Fill with half of ground mixture. Sprinkle with half of nut mixture. Place duck breasts in one layer.

Sprinkle with remaining nut mixture. Cover with remaining ground mixture. Place bay leaves on top. Cover with bacon strips. Cover pan tightly with foil. Place pan in pan of hot water. Bake in preheated 300° oven for 2 hours. Remove pan from hot water. Place weights (bricks or heavy cans) on foil. Let stand overnight. Remove weights and refrigerate pâté. Before serving, cut off all bacon and excess fat. With sharp knife, cut into thin slices and overlap on platter. Garnish with orange halves and watercress. Serve as an appetizer or part of a buffet. Makes 16 to 20 slices.

CODFISH CAKES À LA PORTUGAISE

A spicy dish from the Portuguese of Provincetown.

1 pound salt codfish
1 pound all-purpose potatoes
1 egg
½ teaspoon nutmeg
Freshly ground pepper
5 tablespoons oil
1 medium green pepper, cut in
    1-inch pieces
3 medium stalks celery, cut in
    1-inch pieces

2 medium onions, quartered
3 cloves garlic
1 cup plum tomatoes, chopped
    and drained
½ cup red wine
1 teaspoon hot pepper flakes, or
    to taste
Salt to taste

Soak codfish in cold water overnight, changing water once. Drain. Place in baking dish in water to cover. Cover dish and poach in 350° oven for 25 minutes, until fish flakes. Drain. Boil potatoes until tender. Cool. Peel. Fit processor with METAL BLADE. Combine pieces of fish, quarters of potato and egg. Process 5 seconds. Mixture should retain some texture, not be completely smooth. Turn into bowl. Season with nutmeg and pepper. Shape into 3-inch cakes. Heat 2 tablespoons oil in large skillet. Sauté codfish cakes until golden on both sides. Remove. Process pepper and celery together for 3 seconds. Remove. Process onions and garlic for 3 seconds. Remove. Sauté chopped vegetables in skillet, adding remaining oil. Cook until soft. Add tomatoes and wine, mashing tomatoes with fork. Season with pepper flakes and salt. Simmer for 10 minutes. Spread tomato mixture over bottom of greased 9 x 13-inch baking dish. Arrange codfish cakes on top. Bake in 350° oven for 20 minutes. Garnish with mussels, if desired. Serve with Portuguese bread and a spinach salad. Makes 6 servings.

FISH FILLETS IN SPICY ORANGE SAUCE

*The cold marinade becomes a hot sauce
over sautéed fillets.*

½ cup orange juice
6 tablespoons oil
3 tablespoons coarsely chopped
  onion
¼ cup parsley, stems removed
½ 3-ounce can green chili
  pepper
1 clove garlic

Salt to taste
Freshly ground pepper
2 drops hot pepper sauce
1½ pounds flounder or sole
  fillets
3 tablespoons butter or
  margarine

Fit METAL BLADE into processor. Combine all ingredients in processor except fish and butter. Process 2 seconds. Pour over fish in flat dish. Cover. Marinate fish 2 to 3 hours, turning occasionally. Lift fillets from dish, scraping off excess marinade. Pour marinade into small saucepan. Bring to a boil. Reduce heat to simmer. Heat butter in large skillet. Sauté fish 5 minutes on one side. Turn. Sauté 3 minutes. Remove to serving dish and pour hot sauce over all. Makes 4 servings.

FISHERMAN'S PIE

*A "crust" of mashed potatoes and celeriac gives fish a
new twist.*

¾ pound celeriac (celery root)
2 tablespoons lemon juice
½ pound potatoes, peeled and
  diced
¼ cup milk
2 tablespoons melted butter
Salt to taste
Freshly ground pepper
1 pound white fish (flounder,
  haddock), cut in 1-inch
  squares

2 hardcooked eggs, quartered
2 green onions, white and 2
  inches green, cut in 1-inch
  pieces
1 cup cooked rice
½ cup cream
2 canned plum tomatoes,
  drained

Trim and peel celeriac. Dice and drop into boiling salted water with 1 tablespoon lemon juice. Simmer until tender. Drain. Cook potatoes in boiling salted water with remaining lemon juice until tender. Drain. Heat milk to lukewarm. Fit processor with METAL BLADE. Combine potatoes, celeriac, milk and 1 tablespoon butter in bowl of processor. Process 5 seconds, until smooth. If still lumpy, pulse 3 to 4 times. Remove to bowl and season with salt and pepper. Add diced fish to processor bowl and pulse 5 times, until smooth. Remove to bowl. Add eggs and onions to processor. Pulse 10 times, until finely chopped. Add to fish. Gently stir rice and cream into fish mixture. Season with salt and pepper. Spread fish mixture in greased 9-inch pie pan. Slice tomatoes into strips and arrange in lattice pattern over top. Fit pastry bag with star tube and fill with potato mixture. Pipe over fish in a tic-tac-toe pattern and twice around outside edge. Brush piping with remaining tablespoon of melted butter. Bake in 350° oven for 30 minutes. Serve with glazed carrot slices and a tossed salad. Makes 6 servings.

SALMON PASTIES

Pasty is the Cornish name for a filled pastry. These are very good with a soup and salad, or as a snack. They freeze well.

Pastry:

2½ cups flour

1 cup butter or margarine, divided into 16 pieces

6 tablespoons sour cream

1 egg yolk

½ teaspoon salt

½ teaspoon curry powder

Fit processor with METAL BLADE. Combine all ingredients and process 20 to 30 seconds, until dough forms a ball. Remove, wrap and chill for 30 minutes.

Filling:

2 green onions, sliced

8 mushrooms, quartered

1 tablespoon butter or margarine

1 tablespoon oil

1 7½-ounce can salmon

1 tablespoon fresh or 1 teaspoon dried dillweed

2 hardcooked eggs

½ cup cooked rice

Salt to taste

Freshly ground pepper

1 egg yolk, beaten with 1 tablespoon water

Fit processor with METAL BLADE. Turn onions and mushrooms into processor bowl and pulse 4 to 5 times, until finely chopped. Heat butter and oil in skillet. Sauté mushroom mixture until fairly dry. Pick over salmon and add to processor with dill and eggs. Process 2 seconds. Add to mushroom mixture with rice and seasonings. Stir all together. Roll out pastry on floured board to ¼-inch thickness. Using a small plate as a guide, cut out circles about 6 inches in diameter. Spoon about 3 tablespoons salmon filling across the diameter of each circle. Brush rim with cold water. Bring edges up to meet over filling. Seal by crimping pastry to give a fluted effect. Pasties will resemble half circles standing on their flat sides. Chill 15 minutes or longer. Brush with beaten egg yolk and place on baking sheet. Bake for 10 minutes in preheated 450° oven. Reduce heat to 375° and bake 20 minutes longer, until golden. Makes 6 pasties.

FRUITED HAM LOAF

1 pound ham, cut in 1-inch cubes
1 pound boneless pork, cut in 1-inch cubes
½ small onion, sliced
1 medium tart apple, peeled, cored and quartered
5 pitted prunes
¼ cup parsley, stems removed
2 tablespoons brown sugar, packed

1 egg
1 tablespoon Worcestershire sauce
Salt to taste
Freshly ground pepper
1 teaspoon prepared mustard
2 medium firm, ripe pears, peeled, cored and sliced
⅓ cup chili sauce
2 tablespoons butter or margarine

Fit processor with METAL BLADE. Process ham 6 seconds, half a pound at a time. Remove to bowl. Process pork 6 seconds. Combine with ham. Process onion 3 seconds. Process apples and prunes 3 seconds. Remove to bowl. Add sugar, egg, Worcestershire sauce, salt, pepper and mustard to ham mixture. Mix all together. Form into a loaf and place in baking pan. Bake in preheated 350° oven for 30 minutes. Combine one pear and chili sauce in processor. Process 4 seconds. Spread over top of loaf. Bake 15 minutes longer. Meanwhile, sauté remaining pear slices in butter or margarine for 5 minutes, until glazed. Serve ham loaf garnished with pear slices. Makes 6 servings.

HAM-AND-CHEESE-OMELET SOUFFLÉ

*This may be the quickest and easiest
soufflé on record.*

8 eggs
½ teaspoon salt
½ teaspoon dry mustard

4 ounces cheddar or Parmesan
  cheese
4 ounces ham, in one piece

Fit processor with METAL BLADE. Add eggs, salt and mustard. Process 5 seconds, or until foamy. Remove blade and replace with SHREDDING DISC. Shred cheese and ham into egg mixture. Turn out into well-buttered 9-inch pie pan. Bake in preheated 350° oven for 25 minutes, or until firm and puffy. Serve immediately. Makes 4 servings.

HAMBURGER PIE

Something a little different to do with ground beef.

2 ounces cheddar cheese
1 medium green pepper, seeded
1 medium sweet Spanish onion,
  peeled
6 canned plum tomatoes,
  drained
2 slices bread

1½ pounds round or chuck, cut
  in ½-inch cubes
1 teaspoon Worcestershire sauce
Salt to taste
Freshly ground pepper
1 tablespoon prepared mustard

Fit processor with SHREDDING DISC. Shred cheese. Remove. Fit processor with SLICING DISC. Roll up green pepper tightly and stand on end in feed tube. Slice. Remove. Cut onion to fit feed tube, and slice. Remove. Place tomatoes in feed tube horizontally. Slice. Remove. Fit processor with METAL BLADE. Process bread 3 seconds. Remove to large bowl. Process meat, half pound at a time, for 4 seconds. Remove to bowl with bread crumbs. Add Worcestershire, salt and pepper. Mix well with hands. Divide meat in half. Spread half over bottom of 9-inch round baking pan or cake tin. Spread with mustard. Cover with onion slices, green pepper slices and half of tomato slices. Pat remaining meat over vegetables. Cover with remaining tomatoes. Sprinkle with cheese. Bake in 350° oven for 30 minutes. Serve with pan-fried potatoes and buttered peas. Makes 6 servings.

HUEVOS RANCHEROS

*For those who like hot foods, this is a brisk way
to start the day.*

1 medium onion, quartered
½ red pepper, cut in 1-inch
   pieces
½ medium green pepper, cut in
   1-inch pieces
3 tablespoons oil
2 medium tomatoes, peeled and
   chopped

½–1 teaspoon hot pepper flakes
½ teaspoon ground cumin
4 eggs
4 slices buttered toast or
   tortillas

Fit processor with METAL BLADE. Process onion and pepper for 3 seconds, until finely chopped. Heat oil in large skillet. Sauté onions and peppers until limp. Add tomatoes to skillet, with pepper flakes and cumin. Simmer mixture for 5 minutes. Drop eggs onto sauce. Cover pan and cook over medium heat for 5 minutes, or until eggs are done. Serve eggs on toast or tortillas, with sauce spooned over. Fried bananas go nicely with this dish. Makes 4 servings.

PUFFY CHEESE RING

Ring:
2 ounces Parmesan cheese, cut
   in 1-inch cubes
½ cup butter or margarine
1 cup chicken bouillon or water
½ teaspoon salt

1 cup flour
4 large eggs
1 egg yolk, beaten with
   1 tablespoon water

Fit processor with METAL BLADE. Process cheese 5 seconds. Remove. Place butter, liquid and salt in saucepan. Bring to a full boil. Reduce heat to medium. Add flour all at once and beat with a spoon until mixture forms a smooth shiny ball and leaves a light film over bottom of pan. This will take about 2 minutes. Turn dough into processor. With motor running, add eggs one at a time through feed tube. Process each egg 5 seconds. Add half of cheese. Process 2 seconds. Spread dough on lightly greased baking sheet, shaping a ring 11 inches across, leaving a 7-inch opening in the center.

Brush with egg yolk and sprinkle with remaining cheese. Bake in 375° oven for 45 minutes. Remove and, with the point of a knife, make small slits around the ring. Return to oven for 5 minutes. Remove to rack and cool. Ring will flatten out somewhat.

Filling: Make while ring is baking.

1 10-ounce package frozen leaf spinach	½ pound feta cheese, in pieces
½ small onion, quartered	1 ounce blue cheese, crumbled
2 cups cottage cheese	Freshly ground pepper
	1 egg

Cook spinach, drain and squeeze dry. Fit processor with METAL BLADE. Put spinach into processor with onion. Process 3 seconds. Add cottage cheese, feta cheese and blue cheese. Process 3 seconds. Add pepper and egg. Process 2 seconds. Split ring and place bottom half on ovenproof serving platter. Fill with cheese mixture. Cover with top half and warm in 425° oven for 15 minutes. Serve with avocado-and-citrus salad. Makes 6 servings.

MACARONI TONNATO

This colorful dish can be served as a main course or as part of a buffet. It should be made ahead and left to marinate.

½ cup parsley, stems removed	¼ cup cream
¾ cup oil	¼–½ cup chicken bouillon
1 egg yolk	8 ounces elbow macaroni
1 3-ounce can Italian tuna fish, drained	2 tablespoons capers, drained
4 flat anchovy fillets, drained	Ripe olives
2 tablespoons lemon juice	Lemon slices

Fit processor with METAL BLADE. Process parsley 6 seconds. Remove. Combine ¼ cup oil, egg yolk, tuna fish, anchovy fillets and lemon juice in processor. Process 3 seconds. With motor running, add remaining oil very slowly until mixture thickens. Add cream. Process 2 seconds. Add bouillon until mixture is consistency of heavy cream. Turn out into bowl. Cook macaroni until tender. Rinse. Toss with sauce in bowl. Let stand 2 to 3 hours. Before serving, turn out onto platter. Sprinkle with parsley and capers and garnish with olives and lemon slices. Makes 4 to 6 servings.

MALAY CURRY

Any cooked meat or poultry will do as the main ingredient for this easy, colorful dish.

3 tablespoons oil
2 medium onions
1 rib celery, cut in 1-inch pieces
1 apple, cored and quartered
2–3 teaspoons curry powder
Salt to taste
2 cups chicken broth
3 cups cooked poultry or meat
1 hardcooked egg

1 medium cucumber, peeled, seeded, cut in chunks
½ cup nuts
3 slices cooked bacon
1 small green pepper, seeded, cut in 1-inch pieces
½ cup raisins
1 cup chutney
1 ripe medium banana
Hot rice

Fit processor with SLICING DISC. Add oil to large deep skillet and set over medium heat. Slice onions and add to skillet. Fit processor with METAL BLADE. Process celery 3 seconds, until coarsely chopped. Process apple 3 seconds, until chopped. Add to skillet. Sauté vegetables until soft. Stir in curry powder and salt and cook for 2 minutes. Stir in broth. Add cooked meat or poultry. Cover pan and simmer for 30 minutes. Process egg, cucumber, nuts, bacon and pepper, one at a time, until finely chopped. Put into bowls. Put raisins and chutney into bowls. Just before serving, slice banana by hand and put into bowl. Serve curry with a Cucumber-and-Tomato Raita (see page 104 for recipe) and a fruit dessert. This dish will freeze. Makes 6 servings.

MATAMBRE (STUFFED FLANK STEAK)

An Argentinean dish. The well-deserved name means "to kill hunger."

1 cup broth (we used beef)
¼ cup cider vinegar
1 teaspoon salt
½ teaspoon thyme
¼ teaspoon pepper
1 flank steak (about 1½ pounds), butterflied lengthwise and pounded to ¼-inch thickness

1 slice bread
4 slices bacon, cut in 1-inch pieces
1 medium onion, quartered
2 cloves garlic
2 hardcooked eggs
1 medium carrot
1 10-ounce package frozen chopped spinach, thawed and squeezed dry

In shallow dish, mix broth, vinegar, salt, thyme and pepper. Add steak and, turning occasionally, marinate at least 45 minutes, or refrigerate overnight. Fit processor with METAL BLADE. Process bread 5 seconds. Remove. Process bacon, onion and garlic 10 seconds. Remove to Dutch oven. Sauté until bacon is crisp. Meanwhile, process eggs 3 seconds. Fit processor with SHREDDING DISC. Shred carrot. Remove bacon mixture to clean bowl with slotted spoon, reserving drippings. To bacon mixture add eggs, carrot, spinach and crumbs; mix well. Remove steak from marinade; reserve marinade. Spread steak with spinach mixture to within ½ inch of edge. Starting at narrow end, roll up tight as for jelly roll. Tie securely crosswise, then lengthwise. Brown on all sides in reserved drippings. Add marinade; cover and simmer 1 hour, or until tender. Remove; let stand 10 minutes. This dish can be frozen for 3 to 4 weeks. Makes 6 servings.

MEATBALLS WITH SPICY-SWEET APPLE-ONION SAUCE

Good for just the family or for company dinner.

2 slices white bread
1¼ pounds boneless chuck or round steak
2½ medium onions
⅓ cup milk
1 egg
1 teaspoon salt

Flour
3 tablespoons oil
2 medium apples, cored and quartered
⅓ cup raisins
½ cup cider or apple juice

Sauce:

¾ cup beef bouillon blended with 3 tablespoons cornstarch
¼ cup mayonnaise
1 teaspoon salt

1 teaspoon brown sugar
1 tablespoon vinegar
¼ teaspoon ginger

Fit processor with METAL BLADE. Process bread 10 seconds. Remove to large bowl. Process meat, half a pound at a time, for 5 seconds. Combine with crumbs. Cut up ½ onion and combine with milk and egg in processor. Process 4 seconds. Add to meat mixture with salt. With hands, blend well and form into 1½-inch balls. Dip in flour. Brown in hot oil in large skillet. Meanwhile, fit processor with SLICING DISC. Slice rest of onions and the apples. Add to skillet. Sauté about 5 minutes. Add raisins and cider; cover and cook over low heat about 15 minutes. Remove meatballs and keep warm. Stir sauce ingredients into skillet; cook over low heat until thickened. Add meatballs, spooning on sauce. Serve over rice accompanied with broccoli and hot biscuits. Makes 6 servings.

MOUSSAKA OF TURKEY

2 ounces cheddar or Gruyere
  cheese, cut in 1-inch pieces
1 turkey breast, approximately
  2½ pounds
1 medium onion, quartered
½ cup plum tomatoes, chopped
  and drained
½ cup parsley, stems removed
Salt to taste
Freshly ground pepper

½ teaspoon dried basil
1 pound potatoes
1 pound zucchini, unpeeled
2 tablespoons oil
4 tablespoons butter or
  margarine
4 tablespoons flour
1 cup chicken bouillon
1 cup milk

Fit processor with METAL BLADE. Process cheese 4 seconds. Remove. Remove turkey meat from bones and cut into 1-inch pieces. Process half a pound at a time, 3 seconds, until finely ground. With last batch, add onion. Process 4 seconds. Remove and combine with tomatoes. Process parsley 4 seconds. Mix turkey, salt, pepper and basil. Fit processor with SLICING DISC. Peel potatoes and slice. Slice zucchini. Heat oil in skillet and sauté zucchini until just tender. Heat butter and flour together in saucepan, stirring until blended. Add bouillon and milk. Cook, stirring until smooth and thickened. Stir in cheese. Season to taste. Layer potatoes on bottom of greased 2-quart baking dish. Spread turkey mixture over potatoes. Top with zucchini slices. Pour cheese sauce over all. Bake in 350° oven for 1 hour. Serve with toasted pita bread and a green salad. Makes 6 servings.

OYSTER-AND-SPINACH SHELLS

*Use as an appetizer or a luncheon dish, with
marinated cucumbers and hot rolls.*

1 10-ounce package frozen leaf
  spinach
½ pint shucked oysters
½ small clove garlic
2 tablespoons white wine or
  Vermouth

Salt to taste
Freshly ground pepper
¼ cup heavy cream
1 tablespoon butter or
  margarine
½ teaspoon ground nutmeg

Plate 1/ Malay Curry with garnishes of red peppers,
hard-boiled eggs, green peppers, raisins and chutney.

Plate 2/ *Left to right:* Marinara sauce,
zucchini canoes, cucumber salad mold.

Plate 3/ *Left to right:* Hot roast turkey under wraps,
Matambre (Argentinean stuffed flank steak), boiled pork dinner.

Plate 4/ *Clockwise from top left:* Citrus-avocado salad with
honey and poppy seed dressing, pear-carrot-cheese salad with French
dressing, banana-orange-radish salad with mustard dressing,
apple-kumquat-Chinese cabbage salad with soy dressing.

Plate 5/ *Clockwise from top left:* Green onion loaf,
onion rolls, chili chips, dessert fingers, pizza bread.

Plate 6/ *Clockwise from top left*: Split pea soup,
scotch broth, welsh rarebit and kielbasa soup, garlic soup.

Plate 7/*Clockwise from top left:* German-style vegetable
salad platter, stuffed chayote, braised summer greens.

Plate 8/ *Clockwise from top right:* Apple tart,
coleslaw, Pilgrim lamb stew and whole grain bread.

Cook spinach according to package directions. Drain. Remove any discolored leaves. Squeeze dry. Fit processor with METAL BLADE. Count out 12 oysters and set aside. Put remaining oysters, oyster liquor, garlic and Vermouth into processor bowl. Pulse 3 to 4 times. Add spinach, salt and pepper and process 5 seconds, until mixture is puréed. Divide spinach mixture among 4 ovenproof shells or au gratin dishes. Place 3 oysters on each. Set dishes on baking sheet. Heat cream with butter and nutmeg. Pour over oysters. Bake in preheated 450° oven for 5 to 6 minutes. Serve immediately. Makes 4 servings.

PILGRIM LAMB STEW

*A good, hearty dish that needs just coleslaw and a
fruit dessert to make a complete meal.*

2 medium onions
2 pounds lean lamb, cut in
   1½-inch pieces
1½ cups beef bouillon
Freshly ground pepper
6 medium all-purpose potatoes
1 pound zucchini
4 medium carrots

½ cup white wine
½ cup canned plum tomatoes,
   chopped and drained
1 bay leaf
½ teaspoon thyme
2 sprigs parsley
½ teaspoon rosemary

Fit processor with SLICING DISC. Slice onions. Place lamb, onions, ½ cup bouillon, and pepper in a deep heavy casserole. Place in preheated 325° oven for 1 hour. Peel potatoes and slice. Slice zucchini and carrots. Add remaining bouillon, wine and tomatoes to lamb. Stir in herbs. Layer sliced vegetables in casserole. Cover and cook 1 hour longer. Before serving, mix vegetables and meat together gently. Makes 6 servings.

PRUNE-STUFFED PORK LOIN

8 pitted prunes
3 tablespoons rum
1 medium apple, cored and
   quartered
1 medium stalk celery, cut in
   1-inch lengths
4–5 pound loin of pork

Salt to taste
Freshly ground pepper
1 teaspoon ground rosemary
¼ cup apricot preserves
1 teaspoon ground ginger
3 tablespoons chicken bouillon

Combine prunes with 2 tablespoons rum in saucepan. Simmer until rum is absorbed. Fit processor with METAL BLADE. Process apple and celery for 2 to 3 seconds, until finely chopped. Cut a pocket in the pork loin through its thickest part. Cut down as deep as possible but do not go through to the ends. Line the pocket with the prunes. Fill with apple mixture. Close the top with metal skewers. Sprinkle with salt, pepper and rosemary. Place pork loin on rack in roasting pan. Spread remaining apple mixture over top. Roast in preheated 325° oven for 30 minutes per pound. Combine in processor the apricot preserves, ginger, remaining rum and bouillon. Process for 1 second. After the first hour of roasting, spread half this mixture over meat. Roast 30 minutes longer. Spread remaining mixture over meat. Serve with sweet potatoes and green beans. Makes 6 servings.

RANGE-TOP PORK-APPLE CASSEROLE

Serve with coleslaw and a custard dessert.

1 pound boneless pork shoulder, sliced ⅜ inch thick	2 medium firm cooking apples, cored and quartered
1 tablespoon soy sauce	4 medium (1 pound) potatoes, peeled
½ teaspoon pepper	1 teaspoon salt
1 tablespoon oil	½ teaspoon thyme
1 tablespoon margarine	½ cup water
4 small onions	

Sprinkle pork with soy sauce and pepper. In large heavy skillet, heat oil and margarine. Brown pork well on both sides. Meanwhile, fit processor with SLICING DISC. Slice onions. Remove pork from pan and reserve. Sauté onions in pan drippings, stirring occasionally, until golden brown. Slice apples and potatoes. Add to pan. Add pork. Season with salt and thyme. Add water and bring to boil. Cover and simmer 25 minutes, or until all ingredients are tender. Makes 4 servings.

PORK SOUBISE

Onions and sour cream melt together to make a smooth, rich sauce for pork cutlets.

2½ pound boneless pork, ½ inch thick
⅓ cup flour
Salt to taste
1 teaspoon paprika

¼ cup shortening
6 medium onions
1 cup chicken bouillon
2 cups sour cream
¼ cup parsley, stems removed

Cut pork into 6 serving pieces. Combine flour, salt and paprika. Dredge pork, shaking off excess flour. Heat 2 tablespoons shortening in skillet. Brown pork on all sides. Remove. Fit processor with SLICING DISC. Slice onions. Add remaining shortening to skillet. Add onions. Sauté for 3 minutes, stirring. Add bouillon. Simmer until liquid is absorbed and onions are glossy. Fit processor with METAL BLADE. Put about one-quarter of onions into processor. Process 2 seconds. Add sour cream. Process 5 seconds. Return pork to skillet and cover with sour cream-onion mixture. Cover pan. Simmer over low heat for 1½ hours, until meat is very tender. Process parsley 3 seconds. Remove pork to serving platter, spooning sauce over meat. Sprinkle with parsley. Serve with mashed potatoes and glazed carrots. Makes 6 servings.

STUFFED PORK CHOPS

Good cool-weather fare with baked yams and Brussels sprouts.

6 pork chops, 1 inch thick (approximately 6 ounces each)
2 slices firm white bread
1 small onion, quartered
¼ cup walnuts or pecans
1 medium stalk celery with leaves, cut in ½-inch lengths

¼ cup raisins
Salt to taste
Freshly ground pepper
2 tablespoons shortening
1½ cups cider or apple juice
1 large tart apple

With a sharp knife, cut a pocket in chops 2 to 3 inches long and almost down to the bone. Fit processor with METAL BLADE. Tear up bread and process 5 seconds. Add onion, nuts, celery and raisins to processor bowl. Pulse 4 to 5 times, until ingredients are finely chopped. Turn out into bowl. Stuff chops with mixture and skewer openings. Sprinkle chops on both sides with salt and pepper. In large skillet heat shortening. Brown chops on both sides. Place in baking dish in one layer. Add cider to skillet and bring to a boil. Pour over chops. Cover dish. Bake in 325° oven for 1½ hours, or until chops are very tender. Wash processor bowl and fit with SLICING DISC. Core apple and quarter. Fit pieces into feed tube, cut sides down. Slice. Ten minutes before chops are done, place an apple slice on each chop and finish cooking. Makes 6 servings.

SCALLOPED POTATOES AND SAUSAGE

Serve this hearty dish with Brussels sprouts
and baked applesauce.

2 tablespoons parsley, stems removed	4 large all-purpose potatoes, peeled
4 ounces cheddar or Swiss cheese, cut in 1-inch cubes	1 pound smoked sausage, kielbasa style
½ medium green pepper, seeded, cut in 1-inch pieces	1 egg
½ medium onion, sliced	1½ cups milk
1 clove garlic	Salt to taste
	Freshly ground pepper

Fit processor with METAL BLADE. Process parsley 6 seconds. Remove to small bowl. Process cheese 6 to 7 seconds, until grated. Remove. Process green pepper 3 seconds, until chopped. Add to parsley. Process onion and garlic 3 seconds. Add to parsley mixture. Fit processor with SLICING DISC. Slice potatoes. Slice sausage into rings. In greased 1½-quart baking dish, layer ⅓ of the potatoes. Sprinkle with half the parsley mixture. Cover with half the sausage slices. Sprinkle with ¼ cup cheese. Repeat, ending with a layer of potatoes on top and ½ cup cheese remaining. Beat together egg, milk, salt and pepper. Pour over potatoes. Cover dish and bake in preheated 350° oven for 1 hour. Uncover and sprinkle with remaining cheese. Bake, uncovered, for 30 minutes longer, or until potatoes are tender and most of liquid has been absorbed. Makes 4 to 6 servings.

SAUSAGES IN PEPPER WINE SAUCE

*Accompany this dish with boiled potatoes, pickles
and pots of assorted mustards.*

8 Italian sausages (1½ to 2
  pounds)
1 medium red pepper, seeded,
  cut in 1-inch pieces
1 medium green pepper, seeded,
  cut in 1-inch pieces

1 small onion, quartered
Flour
2 tablespoons butter
2 tablespoons oil
1 cup dry white wine
Freshly ground pepper

Place sausages in skillet and add water to cover. Bring to a simmer and cover pan. Cook for 10 minutes. Meanwhile, fit processor with METAL BLADE. Process peppers 3 seconds. Remove. Process onion 3 seconds. Drain sausages. Dredge with flour. Heat butter and oil in skillet. Brown sausages on all sides. Remove. Add peppers and onion to skillet. Sauté until tender. Add wine and pepper and bring to a boil. Boil until reduced and thickened slightly. Return sausages to skillet and heat through. Serve immediately. Makes 4 servings.

SPARERIBS WITH PLUM SAUCE

3 pounds spareribs, cut into 6
  serving pieces
1 medium onion, cut in wedges
1 tablespoon oil
1 tablespoon cornstarch
¾ cup vinegar

1 tablespoon sugar
1 teaspoon soy sauce
2 pounds fresh plums, pitted
  and quartered
Salt to taste

Arrange spareribs on baking pan and place in 350° oven. Roast for 1 hour. Fit processor with METAL BLADE. Process onion for 4 seconds. Turn into skillet with oil. Sauté until soft. Mix cornstarch with vinegar, sugar and soy sauce. Add to onion. Process plums, half a pound at a time, for 3 seconds. Add to skillet. Add salt. Cook, stirring, until mixture has thickened and plums are tender. Return mixture to processor. Process for 2 seconds. Spoon half of sauce over spareribs after first hour of baking. Then baste with remaining sauce every ten minutes, for 40 minutes longer. Serve with oven-fried potatoes and parslied carrots. Makes 6 servings.

STIFLED STEAK

*The onions melt into a lovely sauce as the meat cooks
slowly until it is fork tender.*

6 tablespoons flour
1 clove garlic
½ teaspoon thyme
⅓ cup parsley, stems removed
Salt to taste
Freshly ground pepper
5 tablespoons oil

1½ pounds round steak
4 large onions, peeled
1 cup beef bouillon
1 cup water
1 teaspoon paprika
1 cup sour cream

Fit processor with METAL BLADE. Combine flour, garlic, thyme, parsley, salt and pepper in processor. Process 3 seconds. Add 1 tablespoon oil. Process 1 second. Turn out onto waxed paper. Cut steak into serving pieces. With mallet or edge of plate, pound flour mixture into meat on both sides. Fit processor with SLICING DISC. Slice onions. Heat 2 tablespoons oil in large skillet. Sauté onions until just soft, about 5 minutes. Remove. Add remaining 2 tablespoons oil to skillet. Brown meat on all sides. Cover meat with onions. Pour into skillet the bouillon and water. Cover pan and simmer for 2 hours, until meat is very tender. Remove meat to serving platter. Add paprika and sour cream to pan. Heat, stirring, until smooth. Pour over meat. Serve with mashed potatoes. Makes 4 servings.

VEGETABLES

Hot and Cold, Soufflés, Entrées, Stir-Fry, Timbales

BRAISED SUMMER GREENS

2 pounds escarole, chard, tender
    turnip or mustard greens
1 small onion
1 large garlic clove
2 tablespoons oil

1 teaspoon salt
½ teaspoon freshly ground
    pepper, or to taste
Onion rings
Vinegar or lemon juice

Wash the greens and dry thoroughly. Fit processor with SLICING DISC. Pack greens
into feed tube. Slice. Remove. Slice onion and garlic. In Dutch oven or kettle, heat oil;
sauté onion and garlic slices 2 to 3 minutes, stirring often. Add greens, tossing just
until wilted. Cover and braise 10 to 25 minutes, or until tender. Season with salt and
pepper. Turn into warm serving dish. Garnish with onion rings. Serve with vinegar.
Makes 4 to 6 servings.

STUFFED CHAYOTE

Chayote, a subtropical squash, is found in Latin markets. It is deeply ribbed, pear shaped and has a greenish-white rind and one seed. If the seed is soft and undeveloped, it may be cooked and eaten with the squash. If hard, discard. If chayotes are not available, use eggplant or other vegetables (squash, green peppers, tomatoes).

2 chayotes (about 1 pound each), split lengthwise
Boiling salted water
3 tablespoons butter or margarine
3 large ribs celery
2 slices bread
1 large onion, cut in quarters
1 large clove garlic, sliced
1 medium-size green pepper, seeded and cut in ½-inch squares

6–8 ounces small shrimps, cooked, shelled, deveined (reserve 4 whole shrimps for garnish) or 1 6-ounce package frozen cooked ready-to-eat shrimps, thawed but undrained
1 teaspoon salt, or to taste
1 large bay leaf, crumbled (½ teaspoon)
¼ teaspoon hot pepper sauce, or to taste
1 tablespoon melted butter or margarine

Place chayotes (with soft seeds if available) in large skillet in about 1 inch boiling salted water; cover and cook until tender, 25 to 30 minutes, turning once or twice. Drain, cut side down, on paper towels; scoop out flesh (and seeds), leaving thick shells. Set aside. Melt butter in skillet or saucepan. Fit processor with SLICING DISC. Slice celery. Remove to pan with butter. Fit processor with METAL BLADE. Process bread slices 8 to 9 seconds. Remove. Combine ¼ cup bread crumbs with 1 tablespoon melted butter. Process onion and garlic 5 to 6 seconds. Add to celery. Process green pepper 4 to 5 seconds. Add to vegetables in pan. Sauté vegetables until tender. Cut cooked chayote flesh into cubes. Process 3 to 4 seconds. Add to vegetables. Pulse shrimps 3 or 4 times. Add to vegetables. Stir in remaining bread crumbs, salt, bay leaf and pepper sauce; mix well. Fill chayote shells. Sprinkle with buttered bread crumbs. Bake in shallow baking pan in preheated 375° oven 25 to 30 minutes, or until hot and crumbs are lightly browned. Makes 4 servings.

ZUCCHINI CANOES

To prepare zucchini, merely wash and cut off ends.

4 ounces Swiss cheese, cut in
   1-inch cubes
½ slice bread
3 slices bacon
6 medium or 8 small zucchini

Boiling water
1 egg, slightly beaten
¼ cup heavy cream
⅛ teaspoon nutmeg
Salt and pepper to taste

Fit processor with SHREDDING DISC. Shred cheese. Remove. Fit processor with METAL BLADE. Process bread 5 seconds. Remove. In skillet, cook bacon until crisp. Drain on paper towels; crumble and set aside (reserve fat in skillet). With teaspoon, hollow out zucchini in canoe shapes, reserving flesh. Blanch "canoes" in water 2 minutes; drain and set aside. Process reserved zucchini flesh 5 seconds. Sauté in bacon fat until crisp-tender; combine with bacon and remaining ingredients except bread crumbs. Sprinkle 1 teaspoon bread crumbs into each canoe. Fill with zucchini mixture. Place in shallow baking dish; pour 1 inch hot water into dish. Bake in 350° oven 30 minutes, or until knife inserted in zucchini mixture comes out clean. Serves 6.

ARTICHOKES IN A HOT BATH

*This spicy dipping sauce for artichokes can also be
used for other vegetables, raw and cooked.*

4 medium artichokes
1 tablespoon lemon juice
2 anchovy fillets
2 cloves garlic

½ cup butter or margarine,
   melted
¼ cup oil
¼ cup walnuts

Trim artichokes, removing stems. Put into saucepan and add water to come about halfway up artichokes. Add 1 tablespoon lemon juice. Cover and cook over medium heat until a leaf can be pulled easily from the bottom of the artichoke—about 40 minutes. (Length of cooking depends on the size of artichoke.) Meanwhile, fit processor with METAL BLADE. Combine remaining ingredients and process for 3 to 4 seconds, until smooth. Remove to heavy saucepan and keep warm over low heat, stirring occasionally. To serve: Place pan of sauce in rack over candle or on hot plate in center of table. Serve artichokes on separate plates. This should be served as a separate course and could be followed by an omelet and salad or broiled chicken and rice. Makes 4 servings.

STUFFED BAKED ARTICHOKES

When artichokes are in season, try this elegant but easy way to serve them—either separately as a first course or as a vegetable.

2 large or 4 small artichokes	½ cup parsley, stems removed
4 tablespoons walnuts	2 3-ounce packages cream
1 clove garlic	cheese, cut in 1-inch pieces
2 tablespoons oil	2 eggs

Trim stems off artichokes and set in saucepan of cold water. Bring to a boil. Reduce heat and cook, covered, for 30 to 40 minutes, depending on size of artichoke. Artichoke is done when a leaf can be pulled easily from the bottom. Remove and drain upside down. When cool enough to handle, split artichoke in half from the top down. With spoon, remove fuzzy choke, leaving a hollow. Fit processor with METAL BLADE. Combine nuts, garlic and oil in processor. Process 5 seconds. Add parsley. Process 5 seconds. Add cream cheese and eggs. Process 7 seconds, or until smooth. Fill artichokes with this mixture. Arrange cut side up in greased baking dish. Bake in 350° oven for 25 minutes. The hollow will hold the sauce in which to dip the leaves. Makes 4 servings.

ASPARAGUS WITH CAESAR DRESSING

When asparagus is in season, we're always looking for new ways to serve it.

2 ounces Parmesan cheese, cut in 1-inch cubes	2 teaspoons Worcestershire sauce
1 large clove garlic	2 tablespoons tarragon vinegar
2 anchovy fillets	2 tablespoons lemon juice
1 teaspoon dry mustard	1 egg yolk
1 teaspoon salt	6 tablespoons oil
Freshly ground pepper	2½ pounds asparagus

Fit processor with METAL BLADE. Process cheese 10 seconds. Remove. Combine remaining ingredients, except oil and asparagus, in processor and process 2 seconds. With motor running, add oil and process 5 seconds, until sauce thickens. Remove.

Trim asparagus and peel stalks with vegetable peeler up to heads. Lay flat in large skillet and cover with salted cold water. Cover and bring to a boil. Boil for 7 to 10 minutes, until thickest stalks are just tender. Drain on towels and serve with sauce and grated cheese over each bundle of asparagus. This is nicest when served as a separate course with French bread. Makes 6 servings.

ASPARAGUS LOAF

*You may use just stems for this, as long as you have
1 cup of asparagus.*

½ pound asparagus, cut in
  1-inch lengths
2 ounces cheddar or Swiss
  cheese, cut in 1-inch cubes
10 saltines, broken up

1 large green onion, white
  part only
2 eggs
1 cup milk
Salt to taste
Freshly ground pepper

Cook asparagus in boiling salted water until very tender. Drain. Fit processor with METAL BLADE. Process cheese 10 seconds. Remove. Process saltines with onion 10 seconds. Remove. Add asparagus and process 5 seconds. Add eggs and milk. Process 3 seconds. Add cheese and saltines and process 2 seconds. Season. Turn into well-greased 7 x 4-inch loaf pan. Bake in 350° oven for 40 to 45 minutes. Let stand at room temperature 10 minutes. Run knife around edges and turn out onto platter. Makes 4 or 5 servings.

ASPARAGUS RISOTTO

*This springtime vegetable dish goes well with a
stuffed roast chicken.*

2 ounces Parmesan cheese, cut
  in 1-inch cubes
½ pound asparagus, cut in
  1-inch lengths
2 green onions

4 tablespoons butter or
  margarine
1 cup uncooked rice
2 cups chicken bouillon
Salt to taste
Freshly ground pepper

Fit processor with METAL BLADE. Process cheese for 10 seconds. Remove. Process asparagus and onions for 4 seconds, until finely chopped. Heat butter in saucepan. Sauté onions and asparagus for 5 minutes. Add rice. Sauté for 2 minutes. Add 1 cup bouillon. Cover pan and cook over medium heat for 10 minutes, or until liquid is almost absorbed. Add ½ cup bouillon. Cook until almost dry. Add remaining bouillon. Cook until rice is tender. Stir in cheese. Season. Makes 4 servings.

BEAN RAGOUT

3 tablespoons parsley, stems removed
1 medium green pepper, seeded, cut in 1-inch squares
1 medium onion, sliced
3 medium ribs celery, cut in 1-inch lengths
3 tablespoons oil
1 ripe tomato, peeled and chopped
1 1-pound can red kidney beans
1 1-pound can white kidney beans
1 tablespoon vinegar
1 tablespoon brown sugar, packed
Salt to taste
Freshly ground pepper

Fit processor with METAL BLADE. Process parsley 7 seconds. Remove. Process green pepper 4 seconds. Remove. Process onion 4 seconds. Remove. Process celery 5 seconds. Remove. Heat oil in large skillet or saucepan. Sauté pepper, onion and celery until soft. Add tomato to pan. Drain and rinse beans. Add to pan. Bring mixture to a boil. Reduce heat and simmer for 30 minutes. Stir in vinegar, sugar, salt and pepper. Simmer for 10 minutes. Sprinkle with parsley. Serve with fried chicken or hamburgers. Makes 6 servings.

BROCCOLI LORRAINE

A main dish or vegetable accompaniment.

4 ounces mozzarella cheese, chilled
2 ounces Swiss or Jarlsberg cheese
2 ounces Parmesan cheese, cut in ½-inch cubes
1 slice bread
3 slices cooked bacon
3 cups cooked broccoli
1 cup cottage cheese
1 egg
1 green onion
Salt to taste
Freshly ground pepper
½ teaspoon nutmeg

Fit processor with SHREDDING DISC. Shred mozzarella. Remove. Shred Swiss. Remove. Fit processor with METAL BLADE. Combine Parmesan, bread and bacon in processor. Process for 6 seconds, until finely grated. Remove. Process broccoli for 8 seconds. Add cottage cheese, egg and onion. Process for 5 seconds. Add seasonings, mozzarella and Swiss cheese. Process for 3 seconds. Turn out into buttered 8-inch round baking dish. Sprinkle crumb mixture over top. Bake in 350° oven for 30 minutes. Serves 4 as an entrée, 6 as a vegetable.

CARROT RING

Fill center with any contrasting vegetable.

2 pounds carrots, cut in 1-inch pieces	1 tablespoon brown sugar, packed
4 eggs	Salt to taste
2 tablespoons melted butter or margarine	Freshly ground pepper
½ cup hot milk	8 ounces cheddar or Jarlsberg cheese
1 teaspoon prepared mustard	1½ cups cooked lima beans
	2 tablespoons chopped chives

Cook carrots in boiling salted water until very tender. Drain. Fit processor with METAL BLADE. Process carrots 15 seconds until smooth, scraping down from sides if necessary. Add eggs, butter, milk, mustard, sugar and seasonings. Process 5 seconds. Fit processor with SHREDDING DISC. Shred cheese into carrot mixture. Turn out into very well-greased 1½-quart ring mold, mixing together gently with spatula. Place mold in pan of hot water. Bake in preheated 350° oven for 40 minutes, until firm. Remove mold from water and let stand 10 minutes. Run knife around edges and turn out onto platter. Fill center with lima beans and sprinkle with chopped chives. Makes 6 to 8 servings.

CAULIFLOWER WITH SAUCE GUSTAV

*A handsome dish for a summer buffet that can be
done ahead.*

1 cup spinach leaves, packed
Leaves of ½ bunch watercress
1 cup parsley, stems removed
4 green onions, sliced
1 clove garlic, sliced
2 teaspoons dry mustard
1 egg yolk

1½ teaspoons vinegar
3 tablespoons lemon juice
Salt to taste
Freshly ground pepper
1¼ cups mayonnaise
¾ cup sour cream
1 medium head cauliflower

Fit processor with SHREDDING DISC. Shred spinach. Fit processor with METAL BLADE. Combine watercress, parsley, onions and garlic. Process for 10 seconds. Add mustard, egg yolk, vinegar and half of lemon juice. Process 4 seconds. Add salt, pepper, mayonnaise and sour cream. Process 5 seconds, until blended. Cook cauliflower until tender but not mushy. Drain and sprinkle with remaining lemon juice. When cauliflower is room temperature, place on serving platter. Pour half of sauce over it. Surround with tomato wedges and marinated green beans or broccoli flowers. Serve remaining sauce in sauceboat. Makes 6 to 8 servings.

CONFETTI RICE

*Chopped vegetables perk up that simple dish of rice
we serve so often.*

2 cups cooked rice
1 small carrot, cut in 1-inch
   slices
1 medium stalk celery, cut in
   1-inch lengths
¼ medium green pepper, cut
   in 1-inch pieces

¼ red pepper, cut in 1-inch
   pieces
2 tablespoons butter or
   margarine
2 tablespoons oil

Spoon rice into strainer or colander and set over hot water. Cover pan and steam rice for 30 minutes or longer. Fit processor with METAL BLADE. Pulse each vegetable 5 times, or until finely chopped. Heat butter and oil in skillet. Sauté vegetables for 8 to 10 minutes, until soft but not shapeless. To serve: Combine two mixtures, adding salt to taste. Makes 4 servings.

GOLDEN GATE STIR FRY

A pretty vegetable combination to brighten up the dinner plate.

½ pound mushrooms
1 sweet red or green pepper, seeded
1 medium onion
2 medium ribs celery
3 tablespoons oil, preferably peanut

1 9-ounce package frozen cut green beans
1 pound fresh bean sprouts, or 2 16-ounce cans, well drained
¼ cup soy sauce
Chow mein noodles

Fit processor with SLICING DISC. Arrange mushrooms in feed tube and slice. Remove. Roll pepper tightly and stand in feed tube. Slice. Remove. Slice onion. Slice celery. Remove. In very large skillet or wok, heat oil. Add green beans, bean sprouts, mushrooms, pepper, onion and celery. Stir fry over high heat, 6 to 8 minutes or until vegetables are just crisp-tender. Stir in soy sauce. Serve sprinkled with chow mein noodles. Makes 6 to 8 servings.

HOT HERBED PILAF

A nutritional, nutty grain dish to serve with poultry or lamb.

1¼ cups beef or chicken bouillon
1 cup bulgar wheat or groats
2 cups parsley, stems removed
3 green onions with 2 inches green part, cut in 1-inch lengths

1 teaspoon thyme
2 tablespoons lemon juice
6 tablespoons oil
3 canned plum tomatoes, chopped, well drained
Salt to taste
Freshly ground pepper

Bring bouillon to a boil in small saucepan. Stir in wheat. Remove from heat and cover. Let stand 30 minutes. Fluff with fork and turn into large bowl. Fit processor with METAL BLADE. Add parsley and onions. Process 5 seconds, until well chopped. Through feed tube add thyme, lemon juice and oil. Process 3 seconds. Combine mixture and tomatoes with pilaf, tossing gently. Season. Let stand 2 to 3 hours. To serve: Remove to lightly oiled baking dish and heat in 350° oven for 30 minutes. Makes 6 servings.

NEAPOLITAN EGGPLANT

An appealing meatless main dish, especially when the vegetables are garden fresh.

8 ounces mozzarella cheese, chilled
4 ounces Parmesan cheese, cut in 1-inch cubes
4 medium tomatoes, peeled and quartered
2 cloves garlic, sliced
1 teaspoon oregano
1 large eggplant
4 tablespoons oil
2 cups cooked rice
Salt to taste
Freshly ground pepper

Fit processor with SLICING DISC. Cut mozzarella to fit feed tube. Slice. Remove. Fit processor with METAL BLADE. Process Parmesan cheese for 7 seconds, until finely grated. Remove. Process tomatoes with garlic and oregano 3 seconds. Peel eggplant (unless it is right from the garden) and slice into rounds ¼ inch thick. Brush 1 tablespoon oil over baking sheet. Arrange eggplant slices on sheet and brush with 1 tablespoon oil. Broil until limp and golden. Turn and repeat. Layer ingredients in 1½-quart baking dish as follows: half of eggplant, rice, salt and pepper, mozzarella, half tomato mixture, remaining eggplant, remaining tomato mixture, Parmesan cheese. Drip remaining oil over top. Bake in 350° oven for 40 minutes. Serve with cucumbers marinated in dill-yogurt dressing, and herbed pita bread. Makes 6 servings.

EGGPLANT ON THE HALF SHELL

1 medium eggplant
1 teaspoon salt
1½ slices bread
3 large garlic cloves, sliced
⅓ cup oil
2 tomatoes, peeled, cut in wedges

Cut unpeeled eggplant in half lengthwise. With sharp knife, make ½-inch cuts over surface. Sprinkle with salt and let stand for 45 minutes. Wipe dry with paper towel. Fit processor with METAL BLADE. Process bread 6 seconds. Add garlic and oil. Process 5 seconds, or until mixture becomes a paste. Spread over cut surfaces of eggplant. Place eggplant halves, crumb sides up, in greased baking dish. Place tomato wedges on eggplant. Pour in water to cover bottom of pan. Bake in 425° oven for 30 to 45 minutes, until tender. Length of baking time depends on age of eggplant. Serve with lamb or chicken. Makes 4 servings.

EGGPLANT PUDDING

This is like a soufflé, but with much more to it. A good accompaniment to chicken or lamb.

1 medium eggplant (about 1 pound)
2 slices bread
4 ounces cheddar or Swiss cheese, cut in 1-inch cubes
1 medium stalk celery, cut in 1-inch lengths

½ medium green pepper, cut in 1-inch pieces
1 medium onion, quartered
1 clove garlic
2 eggs
Salt to taste
Freshly ground pepper
2–3 drops hot pepper sauce

Peel eggplant and cube. Drop into saucepan of salted boiling water. Cook for 10 to 15 minutes, until eggplant is soft. Drain well. Fit processor with METAL BLADE. Process bread 10 seconds. Remove to bowl. Process cheese 5 to 6 seconds. Combine with crumbs. Take out ¼ cup of mixture and set aside. Chop celery, pepper and onion and garlic together by pulsing 3 to 4 times. Add eggplant and eggs to processor and pulse 2 or 3 times, until mixture is fairly smooth. Turn into bowl with crumbs. Season and mix well. Turn into greased 1-quart baking dish. Sprinkle remaining ¼ cup crumbs over top. Bake at 350° for 30 minutes. Makes 6 servings.

EGGPLANT WITH ZUCCHINI SAUCE

1 eggplant, peeled, cut in 1-inch cubes
2 ounces Parmesan cheese
1 slice buttered bread
1 pound zucchini, ends removed
¼ cup butter or margarine

½ onion, sliced
1 clove garlic
1 8-ounce package cream cheese
Salt to taste
Freshly ground pepper

Cook eggplant cubes in boiling salted water until tender, about 12 minutes. Drain. Spread over bottom of greased, shallow 1½-quart baking dish. Fit processor with

METAL BLADE. Process cheese 5 seconds. Add bread. Process 5 seconds, until mixture is finely grated. Remove. Fit processor with SHREDDING DISC. Shred zucchini. Heat butter in large skillet. Add zucchini and sauté over medium-high heat for 5 minutes, stirring. Remove from heat. Fit processor with METAL BLADE. Process onion and garlic 4 seconds. Add cream cheese. Process 4 seconds. Add to zucchini. Return to heat and stir until well blended. Season. Spread over eggplant. Bake in preheated 350° oven for 30 minutes. Makes 6 servings.

EGGPLANT-ZUCCHINI PARMIGIANA

A good, low-calorie, easy and economical
main course.

1 medium (1 pound) eggplant,
    cut in ¼-inch crosswise slices
1 tablespoon mayonnaise-type
    salad dressing
1 slice bread
1 tablespoon parsley, stems
    removed
1 clove garlic, sliced
½ teaspoon oregano

½ teaspoon basil
1 ounce Parmesan cheese
4 ounces part-skim mozzarella
    cheese
1 small (6 ounce) zucchini
1 cup low-fat cottage cheese
1 egg
1 8-ounce can tomato sauce

Fit processor with METAL BLADE. Arrange eggplant in 1 layer on cookie sheet. Spread with dressing. Combine bread, parsley, garlic and herbs. Process 10 seconds. Sprinkle over eggplant slices. Bake in preheated 475° oven 10 minutes. Remove from oven; reduce oven temperature to 375°. Process Parmesan cheese 10 seconds. Remove. Fit processor with SHREDDING DISC. Shred mozzarella. Remove. Fit processor with SLICING DISC. Slice zucchini. Remove. Mix together cottage cheese and egg. In 10 x 6 x 2-inch baking dish sprayed with nonstick coating, layer all the eggplant, half the cottage cheese mixture, sauce, mozzarella and Parmesan. Top with all the zucchini and layers of remaining cottage cheese mixture, tomato sauce, mozzarella and Parmesan. Bake, uncovered, in 375° oven 30 minutes, or until bubbly. Let stand 5 minutes before cutting. Makes 4 servings.

MARINARA SAUCE

Be sure tomatoes are very ripe.

2 medium-size onions	3 quarts finely chopped seeded
2 medium-size green peppers,	peeled tomatoes
cut in ½-inch pieces	2 teaspoons salt
⅔ cup olive oil	1 teaspoon each rosemary,
2 cloves garlic, halved	thyme and basil

Fit processor with SLICING DISC. Slice onions. Remove. Fit processor with METAL BLADE. Process peppers 5 to 7 seconds until coarsely chopped. Remove. Heat oil in large enamel kettle. Add onions and peppers and sauté until onions are tender. Process garlic 3 to 4 seconds. Add to kettle and sauté 3 minutes. Add remaining ingredients. Simmer uncovered over low heat 3 hours or until thick, stirring every 20 minutes. Pour into sterilized 1-pint canning jars, leaving 1-inch headspace; seal. Following manufacturer's directions, process in pressure canner at 15 pounds pressure 25 minutes. (If using a pressure saucepan, add 20 minutes to processing time.) Makes about 5 pints. *NOTE:* If desired, unprocessed sauce may be stored in refrigerator up to 1 week or frozen in airtight containers up to 3 months.

HAM-AND-SPINACH PIE

1 pound ham, well trimmed,	¼ cup cottage cheese
cut in ½-inch cubes	½ teaspoon nutmeg
½ small onion, sliced	Salt to taste
2 eggs	Freshly ground pepper
2 10-ounce packages frozen leaf	½ cup tomato sauce
spinach, cooked and drained	1 tablespoon chopped chives
¼ cup sour cream	

Fit processor with METAL BLADE. Process ham in two batches, 5 seconds each, until finely ground. Remove to bowl. Process onion 4 seconds. Add to ham. Mix ham, onion and 1 egg until well blended. Spread over bottom of 9-inch pie pan. Bake in preheated 350° oven for 10 minutes. Process spinach with remaining egg, sour cream, cottage cheese and seasonings, 5 seconds, until well mixed and chopped. Spread tomato sauce over ham. Sprinkle with chives. Spread spinach mixture over sauce. Bake for 35 to 40 minutes, until firm. Serve at room temperature. Makes 6 servings.

CREAMED MUSHROOMS

*A basic mixture that is good to have on hand for
stuffing, saucing, soups and stews.*

½ pound mushrooms
6 tablespoons butter or
  margarine
2 tablespoons flour

½ cup milk or light cream
½ teaspoon grated nutmeg
Salt to taste
Freshly ground pepper

Fit processor with SLICING DISC. Stack mushrooms on their sides in feed tube. Using gentle pressure, slice mushrooms. Heat butter in large skillet. Sauté mushrooms over medium heat for 5 minutes. Sprinkle flour over mushrooms and cook, stirring, for 2 minutes. Add milk and cook for 5 minutes, until mixture is thickened. Season. You may vary this recipe with the addition of a chopped green onion, a teaspoon of mustard or some chopped herbs, or by using half bouillon as the liquid.

MUSHROOM RICE

An old Southern dish.

1 cup uncooked rice
1 large green onion, sliced
8 large mushrooms, quartered

4 tablespoons butter or
  margarine
Salt to taste
Freshly ground pepper

Cook rice in large pan of boiling salted water for exactly 12 minutes. Drain and rinse. Put rice in strainer over hot water and steam for 30 minutes. Fit processor with METAL BLADE. Combine mushrooms and onion. Pulse 5 to 6 times, until finely chopped. Heat butter in large skillet and add mushroom mixture. Sauté over medium-high heat for 5 minutes, stirring. Remove from heat. Just before serving, combine rice and mushroom mixture and heat through. Season and serve. If you have any rice left over, add it to chicken bouillon for a quick, delicious soup. Makes 6 servings.

TWICE-BAKED ACORN SQUASH

*First you bake it, then you stuff it and
bake it again.*

1 large acorn squash
⅓ pound cheddar cheese, cut in
   1-inch cubes
2 teaspoons ground ginger
4–5 tablespoons beef or chicken
   bouillon

Salt to taste
Freshly ground pepper
2 tablespoons melted butter or
   margarine

Cut squash in half. Place in steamer over hot water. Cover pan and steam over medium heat for 40 minutes, until very soft. (You may also steam squash in covered pan in a 400° oven.) Remove and, when cool enough to handle, scrape out seeds and strings. Fit METAL BLADE into processor. Process cheese 5 to 6 seconds, until finely grated. Scoop out flesh of squash and add to processor. Try not to tear the squash shells. Add ginger, bouillon, salt and pepper to squash. Process 5 seconds, or until smooth. Cut shells in half lengthwise and fill with squash mixture. Place in baking dish. Sprinkle with melted butter. Bake in 350° oven for 30 minutes. Makes 4 servings.

SHERRIED MUSHROOM SOUFFLÉ

*This can be served as a main course or as a
vegetable accompaniment.*

½ pound mushrooms
4 slices buttered bread
3 ounces Jarlsberg cheese, cubed
3 eggs

1 teaspoon dry mustard
½ teaspoon ground nutmeg
1½ cups milk
¼ cup dry sherry

Fit processor with SLICING DISC. Stack mushrooms in feed tube and slice. Remove. Cube bread. Fit processor with METAL BLADE. Grate cheese. Remove. Combine remaining ingredients in processor. Process 4 seconds. Place half the mushrooms in buttered 1-quart soufflé dish. Cover with half the bread, then half the cheese. Repeat. Pour in milk mixture. Let stand for at least 1 hour. Bake in preheated 350° oven for 40 minutes, until firm and puffy. Makes 4 or 5 servings.

BAKED GOLDEN ONIONS

*Elevating the onion to epicurean heights is easy
with this foolproof recipe.*

6 large yellow onions
2 slices bread
3 tablespoons melted butter

½ teaspoon paprika
¼ cup tomato juice or chili
  sauce
¼ cup honey

Peel onions and cut in half across. Place in one layer in buttered baking dish. Fit processor with METAL BLADE. Process bread 6 seconds. Add remaining ingredients and process 4 seconds. Spread over cut surfaces of onions. Cover dish. Bake in 350° oven for 30 to 40 minutes, until tender. Makes 6 to 8 servings.

ONIONS AU GRATIN

Who said onions were a dull vegetable?

1 slice bread
3 tablespoons butter or
  margarine
4 medium onions, peeled

2 eggs
½ cup light cream
Salt to taste
1 teaspoon cumin

Fit processor with METAL BLADE. Process bread 4 seconds with 1 tablespoon butter. Remove. Fit processor with SLICING DISC. Slice onions. Heat remaining 2 tablespoons butter in large skillet. Add onions and sauté for 2 minutes, stirring. Cover pan. Reduce heat and simmer for 15 minutes, until soft. Turn into buttered 8- or 9-inch baking dish. Beat together the eggs, cream, salt and cumin. Pour over onions. Sprinkle crumbs over top. Bake in 350° oven for 25 minutes. Makes 4 servings.

ONION CHEESE TART

Serve hot from the oven, or at room temperature.

3 ounces Parmesan cheese
1½ pounds sweet Spanish
   onions
2 tablespoons parsley, stems
   removed
6 tablespoons solid shortening
1¼ cups flour
½ teaspoon salt
2−3 tablespoons ice water

½ teaspoon prepared mustard
4 tablespoons butter or
   margarine
½ cup chicken bouillon
3 eggs
1 cup sour cream
Salt to taste
2−3 drops hot pepper sauce

Fit processor with SHREDDING DISC. Shred cheese. Remove. Fit processor with SLICING DISC. Slice onions. Remove and wipe out bowl. Fit processor with METAL BLADE. Process parsley 5 seconds. Add shortening, flour and salt. Process 6 seconds, until crumbly. Add 2 tablespoons water. Process 20 seconds, or until pastry forms a ball around spindle. Add more water if necessary, a few drops at a time. Wrap pastry and chill for at least 30 minutes. Roll out and fit into 9-inch pie pan. Bake in preheated 425° oven for 8 minutes. Remove and brush with prepared mustard. Return to oven for 2 minutes. Cool. Heat butter in large skillet. Sauté onions 3 to 4 minutes. Add bouillon. Lower heat. Cover pan and simmer for 15 minutes, until soft and glazed. With slotted spoon, remove half of onions to pie shell. Sprinkle with half of cheese. Repeat with remaining onions and cheese. Combine eggs, sour cream, salt and hot pepper sauce in processor. Process 3 minutes. Spread over filling in pie shell. Place pan on baking sheet. Bake in preheated 350° oven 30 to 35 minutes, until set and puffy. Let stand 10 minutes before slicing. Makes 6 servings.

ST. PATRICK'S DAY PASTA

This pasta wears green in the form of bright pea sauce,
touched up with ham and cheese.

4 ounces ham, cut in 1-inch
    cubes
4 ounces Swiss cheese, cut in
    1-inch cubes
1 10-ounce package frozen peas
½ cup milk

Salt to taste
1 pound thin spaghetti
2 green onions, sliced
¼ cup cream
2 tablespoons parsley, stems
    removed
Freshly ground pepper

Fit processor with METAL BLADE. Process ham for 5 seconds. Remove. Process cheese for 5 seconds. Remove. Cook peas with milk and salt until tender. Cook spaghetti until al dente or just tender. Combine peas, onions, cream, parsley and pepper in processor. Process 15 seconds, or until smooth. Toss hot spaghetti with pea sauce. Sprinkle with ham and cheese and toss again. Serve immediately, with garlic French bread and sliced cucumbers vinaigrette. Makes 6 servings.

PEAS À LA FRANÇAISE

Make sure you serve the lettuce along with the peas.
It is important to the flavor of the dish.

¼ cup parsley, stems removed
½ medium onion, quartered
1 can water chestnuts, drained
6 lettuce leaves, preferably
    Boston or Bibb, not iceberg

3 tablespoons butter or
    margarine
2 10-ounce packages tiny peas
Salt to taste
Freshly ground pepper
½ teaspoon thyme

Fit processor with METAL BLADE. Process parsley 6 seconds. Remove. Process onion 3 seconds. Remove. Fit processor with SLICING DISC. Slice water chestnuts. Remove. Slice lettuce leaves. Heat butter to bubbling in saucepan. Add onion, peas, salt, pepper and thyme. Put lettuce in strainer and rinse under cold water. Place over peas. Cover pan and cook over medium high heat for 5 to 6 minutes, until peas are tender. Stir in water chestnuts and parsley. Raise heat and boil until excess moisture has evaporated. Serve immediately. Makes 6 servings.

DANISH POTATO BAKE

An unusual contrast in flavor and texture makes this casserole a good accompaniment to pork or ham.

6 medium all-purpose potatoes
2 medium stalks celery
1 firm medium apple, peeled,
    cored and quartered
4 tablespoons vinegar

3 tablespoons oil
1 clove garlic
Salt to taste
¾ cup plain yogurt
2 ounces Danish blue cheese

Fit processor with SLICING DISC. Peel potatoes and slice. Cook in boiling, salted water until tender. Drain. Spread over bottom of greased shallow baking dish. Slice celery. Slice apple. Scatter slices over potatoes. Fit processor with METAL BLADE. Combine vinegar, oil, garlic, salt and yogurt in processor. Process for 2 seconds. Remove METAL BLADE. Replace with SHREDDING DISC. Shred cheese. Turn mixture out and spread over vegetables. Bake in 350° oven for 30 minutes. Let stand 5 minutes before serving. Makes 6 servings.

NEW POTATOES IN PEPPER SAUCE

12 medium new red potatoes
2 medium onions
1 medium green pepper
1 medium red pepper
2 tablespoons butter

2 tablespoons oil
½ cup chicken bouillon
Salt to taste
Freshly ground pepper
1 ounce Jarlsberg cheese

With a vegetable peeler, cut out a strip of skin around the middle of each potato. Boil potatoes until tender in salted water. Drain and return to pan. Shake over heat for 2 to 3 minutes to dry. Turn into greased baking dish. Fit processor with SLICING DISC. Slice onions and peppers. Heat butter and oil in large skillet. Sauté onions and peppers for 3 minutes. Add bouillon and simmer for 10 minutes. Season with salt and pepper. Fit processor with SHREDDING DISC. Shred cheese. Spoon vegetables over potatoes and sprinkle with cheese. Heat in 350° oven for 20 minutes. Serve with meat loaf or grilled sausages. Makes 4 servings.

NORMANDY POTATOES

1 pound small red-skinned
  potatoes
½ cup chicken bouillon
½ cup oil
3 tablespoons vinegar
Salt to taste

Freshly ground pepper
½ pound mushrooms
½ green pepper
1 large green onion
½ cup parsley, stems removed

Fit processor with SLICING DISC. Slice potatoes. Remove to saucepan. Barely cover with salted water, and cook until just tender. Do not overcook; potatoes must be firm and slightly underdone. Drain. Place in baking dish. Combine bouillon, oil, vinegar, salt and pepper. Pour over potatoes. Bake in 350° oven for 20 minutes. Slice mushrooms. Fit processor with METAL BLADE. Combine green pepper, onion and parsley. Process for 5 seconds. Layer potatoes, mushrooms and parsley mixture in glass bowl. Let stand 2 to 3 hours. Serve at room temperature. Makes 6 servings.

SPICY SWEET POTATO PUDDING

*This is served as a vegetable accompaniment
to ham or turkey.*

4 medium sweet potatoes
2 eggs
¼ cup orange juice
4 tablespoons melted butter or
  margarine
½ teaspoon cinnamon

½ teaspoon ginger
Salt to taste
Freshly ground pepper
1 tart medium apple, cored and
  peeled

Boil sweet potatoes until tender. Peel. Fit processor with METAL BLADE. Cut potatoes in chunks and add to processor. Process 5 seconds, until mixture is smooth. Add eggs, orange juice, butter, spices and seasonings. Process 5 seconds. Replace blade with SHREDDING DISC. Cut apple in pieces to fit feed tube. Shred into potato mixture. Turn into greased 1-quart baking dish. Stir to mix apple and potato. Bake for 30 minutes in preheated 375° oven. Makes 4 servings.

STUFFED POTATO PANCAKE

*This hearty dish can be an attractive main course
when surrounded by broiled tomatoes and buttered
green peas.*

½ cup parsley, stems removed
½ cup snipped fresh dill weed
　or 1 tablespoon dried
4 ounces mozzarella cheese,
　chilled
3 medium potatoes, peeled and
　cut to fit feed tube
1 large onion, peeled and
　quartered

3 eggs
3 tablespoons flour
6 tablespoons melted butter
　or margarine
Salt to taste
Freshly ground pepper
Creamed Mushrooms (recipe on
　page 85)

Fit processor with METAL BLADE. Process parsley and dill for 3 seconds. Remove BLADE and attach SHREDDING DISC. Shred mozzarella. Remove. Shred potatoes and onion. Turn mixture into large bowl. Replace DISC with METAL BLADE. Add eggs, flour and 2 tablespoons butter to processor. Process 1 second. Add to potato mixture and stir all together, blending well. Season. Heat 1 tablespoon butter in 9-inch skillet. (A nonstick skillet works well here.) Spread half of pancake mixture over pan. Cook over medium heat 3 to 4 minutes, until golden crust has formed on underside. Place plate over skillet and turn pancake out, cooked side up. Add 1 tablespoon butter to skillet. Slide pancake back into pan and cook 3 to 4 minutes longer. Slide out onto plate. Repeat with remaining potato mixture. To serve: Place one pancake in ovenproof dish. Cover with 2 cups Creamed Mushrooms. Cover mushrooms with second pancake. Sprinkle top with cheese. Heat in 350° oven for 25 to 30 minutes, until cheese is melted. Makes 4 servings as an entrée, 6 servings as a vegetable.

SUMMER POTATO SCALLOP

*A casserole that's right from the garden and will act
as a main course or a vegetable accompaniment to the
barbecued burger.*

2 ounces Parmesan cheese, cut
  in 1-inch cubes
4 ounces Jarlsberg or Havarti
  cheese
1½ pounds new potatoes,
  scrubbed
1 cup fresh corn kernels

1 cup milk
2 eggs
¼ cup parsley, stems removed
Salt to taste
Freshly ground pepper
2 medium tomatoes, peeled and
  sliced

Fit processor with METAL BLADE. Grate Parmesan cheese. Remove. Fit processor
with SLICING DISC. Cut Jarlsberg to fit feed tube. Slice. Remove. Cut potatoes to fit
feed tube. Slice. Remove. Fit processor with METAL BLADE. Combine corn, milk,
eggs and parsley in processor. Process 20 seconds. In greased 1½-quart baking dish,
place half of potatoes. Sprinkle with salt and pepper. Cover with tomato slices. Cover
tomato with cheese slices. Finish with remaining potato slices. Season. Pour corn
mixture over all. Sprinkle grated Parmesan on top. Bake in 350° oven for 50 to 60
minutes, until potatoes are tender. Makes 6 servings.

CHEESE-SQUASH CASSEROLE

*This could easily be a main dish with baked onions,
sautéed apple rings and a spinach salad.*

1 pound winter squash, peeled
  and cubed
½ small onion, sliced
1 cup heavy cream
16 soda crackers, broken up

12 ounces ham, cut in 1-inch
  cubes
8 ounces cheddar cheese, cut in
  1-inch cubes
4 eggs
2 tablespoons butter or
  margarine

Cook squash in boiling salted water until tender. Fit processor with METAL BLADE. Process onion 3 seconds. Scald cream with onion in small saucepan. Process crackers 15 seconds, until finely crumbled. Remove. Process ham 5 seconds. Remove. Process cheese 6 seconds. Remove. Drain squash. Turn into processor and process 7 seconds, until fairly smooth. Add cream-onion mixture. Process 5 seconds. Add eggs, 1½ cups cheddar, and ham. Process 5 seconds. Turn into greased 1½- or 2-quart casserole. Sprinkle with crackers and remaining ½ cup cheddar. Dot with butter. Bake in preheated 350° oven 50 minutes, or until lightly browned and bubbly. Makes 6 servings.

HUBBARD SQUASH PUDDING

1 pound hubbard, butternut or any winter squash	¼ cup brown sugar, packed
3 eggs	½ teaspoon cinnamon
2 tablespoons melted butter or margarine	½ teaspoon ginger
	1¼-inch slice orange with peel, seeded

Peel squash and cut into lengths to fit feed tube. Fit processor with METAL BLADE. Add eggs, butter, sugar, spices and orange slice to processor. Process for 9 seconds, until well mixed. Fit processor with SHREDDING DISC. Shred squash. Turn out mixture into buttered 1-quart baking dish. Stir with spoon until blended. Bake in 375° oven for 40 minutes, until knife inserted in center comes out clean. Makes 4 servings.

SPAGHETTI SQUASH WITH SAVORY HAM-NUT TOPPING

1 spaghetti squash (about 3 pounds)	1 large clove garlic, sliced
Water	2 tablespoons oil
Salt	4 ounces ham, cut in 1-inch pieces
2 tablespoons parsley, stems removed	¼ cup walnuts
	1 ounce feta cheese, diced

Put squash into large pot and cover with boiling water. Cook for 10 minutes, turning once. Remove, and halve lengthwise. Discard seeds and strings. Place cut side down in pot with 2 inches salted boiling water. Simmer, covered, for 15 minutes or until tender. Do not overcook or squash will get soggy. Meanwhile, fit processor with METAL BLADE. Process parsley 8 seconds. Remove. Process garlic 2 seconds. Remove to skillet with oil. Sauté for 3 minutes. Process ham 2 seconds. Add to skillet. Process nuts and cheese for 3 seconds. Add to skillet. Cook mixture for 2 to 3 minutes. Fluff up squash pulp with fork and toss with ham mixture. Sprinkle with parsley. Makes 4 servings.

SPINACH-AND-MUSHROOM SOUFFLÉ

2 ounces Parmesan cheese, cut in ½-inch pieces
½ pound mushrooms, quartered
1 10-ounce package frozen leaf spinach
5 tablespoons butter or margarine
4 tablespoons flour
¾ cup milk
½ cup chicken bouillon
Salt to taste
Freshly ground pepper
½ teaspoon nutmeg
5 egg yolks
6 egg whites

Fit processor with METAL BLADE. Process cheese for 8 seconds, until finely grated. Remove. Process mushrooms, 1 cup at a time, for 3 seconds, until finely chopped. Remove. Cook spinach and squeeze dry. Process for 2 seconds, until finely chopped. Heat 2 tablespoons butter in skillet. Add mushrooms and sauté over medium-high heat for 5 minutes. Sprinkle with 1 tablespoon flour. Cook for 2 minutes. Add ¼ cup milk and cook until mixture is thick and smooth. Season with salt and pepper. Heat remaining 3 tablespoons butter with 3 tablespoons flour in saucepan. Cook until golden and bubbly. Add remaining ½ cup milk and bouillon. Cook, stirring, until thick and smooth. Season with salt, pepper and nutmeg. Add egg yolks, one at a time, blending well. Divide mixture in half. Add ½ cup mushroom mixture to one half and spinach to other half. Beat egg whites until stiff. Fold half into mushroom mixture and half into spinach mixture. Butter a 2-quart soufflé dish. Put spinach mixture on bottom. Sprinkle with half of cheese. Top with mushroom mixture. Sprinkle with remaining cheese. Bake in 375° oven for 35 minutes, until soufflé is firm and puffy. Serve immediately. Makes 6 servings.

SPINACH TORTE

*A good use for a small amount of leftover meat,
fish or chicken.*

4 ounces cheddar cheese, cut in
  1-inch cubes
2 ounces Parmesan cheese, cut
  in 1-inch cubes
½ slice bread
½ cup cooked chicken, or any
  meat, in ½-inch pieces

1 10-ounce package frozen
  spinach, cooked and drained
¼ cup white wine
4 eggs
Salt to taste
Freshly ground pepper
½ teaspoon nutmeg

Fit processor with METAL BLADE. Process cheddar cheese for 5 seconds. Remove to bowl. Process Parmesan for 5 seconds. Remove to small bowl. Process bread for 5 seconds. Combine with cheddar. Process chicken for 3 seconds. Remove to bowl with cheddar. Process spinach for 2 seconds. Add wine, eggs, salt, pepper and nutmeg. Process 2 seconds. Combine with cheddar mixture, mixing all together. Spread in buttered 9-inch baking pan. Sprinkle Parmesan over top. Bake 35 to 40 minutes, until set. Let stand 10 minutes before serving. Makes 4 servings.

MIXED VEGETABLE TOSSUP

A dish that is as pretty as a spring bouquet.

½ pound zucchini, unpeeled
½ pound carrots
½ pound white turnips

½ cup parsley, stems removed
¼ cup snipped dill weed
1 cup French dressing

Trim vegetables and peel if necessary. Cut in pieces to fit feed tube. Fit processor with SHREDDING DISC. Shred each vegetable separately and remove to large bowl. Fit processor with METAL BLADE. Process parsley and dill 5 seconds. Heat dressing. Pour sauce over combined vegetables and toss, mixing well. Sprinkle parsley and dill on top. Serve immediately. Makes 6 servings.

ORANGE BAKED YAMS AND APPLES

The perfect accompaniment to a ham loaf.

8 medium yams, peeled
2 large, tart apples, peeled,
  cored and quartered
Peel of ½ orange
4 tablespoons brown sugar,
  packed
½ teaspoon nutmeg

1 teaspoon cinnamon
¼ teaspoon ginger
Salt to taste
6 tablespoons butter or
  margarine
½ cup orange juice

Fit processor with SLICING DISC. Cut yams to fit feed tube, and slice. Remove. Place apple quarters, cut side down, in feed tube and slice. Arrange half of yams on bottom of greased 9 x 13-inch baking dish. Fit processor with METAL BLADE. Combine orange peel, sugar, spices and salt. Process 10 seconds, until peel is finely chopped. Add butter and process 5 seconds. Dot ⅓ of mixture over yams. Cover with apple slices. Dot with ⅓ of butter mixture. Top with remaining yams and remainder of butter mixture. Pour orange juice over all. Cover and bake in preheated 400° oven for 1 hour. Uncover and bake until top potato slices are tender. Makes 6 servings.

A MOUSSE OF ZUCCHINI

2 pounds zucchini, unpeeled
1 large Spanish onion
1 clove garlic
4 tablespoons butter or
  margarine

1 slice bread
1 ounce Romano cheese
Salt to taste
Freshly ground pepper
½ teaspoon oregano

Fit processor with SLICING DISC. Slice zucchini. Turn into saucepan and barely cover with boiling salted water. Cook until just tender. Drain. Slice onion and garlic. Heat butter in large skillet. Sauté onion and garlic until soft. Fit processor with METAL BLADE. Process bread and cheese for 10 seconds. Remove. Process zucchini and onion mixture 7 to 8 seconds. Add seasoning. Turn into greased 1½-quart baking dish. Spread crumbs over top. Bake in preheated 350° oven for 15 minutes. Makes 6 servings.

ZUCCHINI-WALNUT SOUFFLÉ

*Zucchini, walnuts and feta cheese combine to make a
tasty and unusual vegetable dish.*

½ pound zucchini (1 medium)
1 tablespoon oil
¼ cup walnuts
1 clove garlic, sliced
¼ pound feta cheese

5 egg yolks
6 egg whites
Salt to taste
Freshly ground pepper

Fit processor with SHREDDING DISC. Shred zucchini and turn into colander. Sprinkle with 1 teaspoon salt. Let stand for 30 minutes. Squeeze dry with hands. Heat oil in skillet. Add zucchini. Sauté over high heat for 3 to 4 minutes to dry out. Fit processor with METAL BLADE. Chop walnuts fine. Remove to bowl. Combine zucchini, garlic, cheese and yolks. Process 5 seconds. Turn out into bowl. Stir together with walnuts. Season. Beat whites until stiff and fold into zucchini mixture. Turn into greased 1½-quart soufflé dish. Bake in 350° oven for 40 minutes, until firm and puffed. Makes 4 servings.

SALADS

Vegetable, Fruit, Molded

APPLE-AND-BLUE CHEESE SALAD

A crunchy combination.

¼ cup walnuts or pecans
2 medium ribs celery
2 large red eating apples, cored
  and quartered
½ cup sour cream
¼ cup mayonnaise

1 ounce blue cheese
1 tablespoon lemon juice
¼ teaspoon celery salt
⅛ teaspoon pepper
Greens (optional)

Fit processor with METAL BLADE. Process nuts 3 seconds. Remove. Fit processor with SLICING DISC. Stand celery ribs upright in feed tube and slice. Place apple quarters, cut side down, in feed tube and slice. Remove celery and apples to large bowl. Fit processor with METAL BLADE. Add remaining ingredients. Process 4 seconds, until blended. Toss with apple mixture. Sprinkle with nuts; serve on greens. Makes 4 servings.

AVOCADO-BLUE CHEESE RING

A good contrast of color, texture and flavor, especially with tomato garnish.

Cheese ring:

1 package unflavored gelatin	2 ounces blue cheese
½ cup white wine or vermouth	8 ounces cream cheese
2 tablespoons parsley, stems removed	½ cup mayonnaise
	½ cup buttermilk
¼ small onion	Salt to taste

Soak gelatin in ¼ cup wine. Fit processor with METAL BLADE. Process parsley and onion for 3 seconds. Heat remaining ¼ cup wine and dissolve gelatin. Replace METAL BLADE with PLASTIC BLADE. Add cheese, cut into sections, and process 5 seconds. Add mayonnaise, buttermilk and gelatin mixture. Process 5 seconds. Add salt. Process 1 second. Turn into 6-cup ring mold. Chill until set.

Avocado ring:

1 package unflavored gelatin	½ cup mayonnaise
1 cup chicken bouillon	Salt to taste
1 ripe avocado	Salad greens (optional)
1 teaspoon lemon juice	Tomatoes, diced (optional)
2–3 drops hot pepper sauce	

Soak gelatin in ¼ cup bouillon. Heat remaining bouillon and dissolve gelatin. Fit processor with METAL BLADE. Process avocado for 5 seconds, stopping machine to scrape down sides. Add gelatin, lemon juice, hot pepper sauce, mayonnaise and salt. Process 3 seconds, until smooth. Turn into mold over cheese ring. Chill overnight. Turn out and surround with greens. Fill center with diced tomatoes. Makes 6 servings.

GINGER-LIME-CUCUMBER MOLD

1 small onion, quartered	1 cup ginger ale
2 cucumbers, peeled, seeded, diced	8 ounces cream cheese
1 package lime gelatin	1 cup mayonnaise
¼ cup cold water	2 tablespoons lemon juice
	½ teaspoon salt

Fit processor with METAL BLADE. Process onion 2 seconds. Add cucumbers. Process 5 seconds until finely chopped. Remove. Soak gelatin in cold water. Heat ginger ale and melt gelatin in it. Fit processor with PLASTIC BLADE. Combine cream cheese, gelatin mixture, mayonnaise, lemon juice and salt. Process 10 seconds until smooth. Add cucumbers and onion. Process 3 seconds. Turn into ring mold. Chill overnight. Unmold on greens. Serve with mayonnaise. Makes 6 to 8 servings.

CAPONATA

A spicy eggplant mixture that can be served as a salad, a vegetable or an appetizer, on dark bread.

¼ cup parsley, stems removed
2 tablespoons walnuts
2 medium eggplants
¾ cup oil
1 large tomato, peeled and
   quartered
2 stalks celery
6 pitted black olives

2 medium onions
¼ cup capers, drained
¼ cup vinegar
2 tablespoons sugar
¼ cup raisins
Salt to taste
Freshly ground pepper

Fit processor with METAL BLADE. Process parsley and nuts for 3 seconds. Remove. Peel eggplant and dice. Process, 1 cup at a time, for 3 seconds. Heat ½ cup oil in large skillet and sauté eggplant until soft and lightly browned. Process tomato and celery for 3 to 4 seconds. Remove. Process olives for 2 seconds. Remove. Fit processor with SLICING DISC. Slice onions. Remove eggplant from skillet. Add remaining ¼ cup oil. Sauté onions until soft. Add tomato and celery and cook until celery is tender. Add capers, parsley, nuts, olives and eggplant. Heat vinegar with sugar and raisins until sugar is dissolved. Add to skillet. Season with salt and pepper. Simmer for 20 to 30 minutes, stirring frequently. Cool to room temperature before serving. This is better when made a day ahead. Makes 6 to 8 servings.

CELERY SLAW

Colorful, crunchy and cool.

8 medium stalks celery
1 medium red pepper, cut in
  1-inch pieces
1 medium green pepper, cut in
  1-inch pieces
½ cup plain yogurt

¼ cup oil
2 tablespoons vinegar
1 tablespoon sugar
1 tablespoon celery seed
Salt to taste
Freshly ground pepper

Cut celery in lengths to stand vertically in feed tube. Fit processor with SLICING DISC. Stack celery in feed tube and slice. Turn into large bowl. Fit processor with METAL BLADE. Process peppers in 2 batches for 4 seconds each. Add to celery. Combine yogurt, oil, vinegar, sugar and seasonings in processor. Process 3 seconds. Pour over vegetables and toss all together. Chill. Makes 6 servings.

CREAMY MOLDED FRUIT SALAD

A good luncheon dish, with hot muffins.

1 envelope unflavored gelatin
3 tablespoons water
½ cup orange juice
1 8-ounce package cream
  cheese, in 4 pieces
2 tablespoons sugar
¼ teaspoon salt
½ cup mayonnaise

½ cup heavy cream, whipped
Salad greens
2 medium peaches
2 small bananas
1 cup pitted black cherries
1 tablespoon lemon juice
1 tablespoon orange juice

Fit processor with METAL BLADE. Add water to processor bowl. Sprinkle gelatin over water. Heat orange juice. With motor running, pour orange juice through feed tube. Fit processor with PLASTIC BLADE. Add cream cheese, sugar, salt and mayonnaise. Process for 5 seconds, until smooth and creamy. Add whipped cream and process 3 seconds. Turn into lightly oiled 5-cup ring mold. Chill overnight. Unmold onto platter and garnish with greens. Peel and quarter peaches. Fit processor with SLICING DISC. Placing peach quarters cut side down in feed tube, slice peaches. Peel and slice bananas by hand. Toss fruits with cherries in fruit juices. Fill center of ring and spoon fruit around edge in small bunches. Makes 6 to 8 servings.

CRUNCHY SALAD

A salad with texture, made from the winter roots and fruits.

1 medium white turnip, peeled
1 medium apple, cored and
    quartered
2 large celery stalks, cut in
    3-inch lengths
½ medium red onion, peeled

½ cup mayonnaise
½ cup sour cream
1 teaspoon mustard
1 tablespoon sugar
1 teaspoon celery seed
Freshly ground pepper

Fit processor with SLICING BLADE. Cut turnip to fit feed tube. Slice. Insert apple in feed tube, cut side down. Slice. Slice celery. Slice onion. Turn out into salad bowl. Fit processor with METAL BLADE. Combine remaining ingredients and process 3 seconds. Mix into sliced vegetables. Let stand 2 to 3 hours. Makes 4 servings.

CUCUMBER-AND-TOMATO RAITA

A soothing accompaniment to spicy curry.

1 large cucumber, peeled,
    seeded, cut in chunks
1 tomato, peeled, seeded,
    quartered

2 cups plain yogurt
½ teaspoon ground cumin
Freshly ground pepper
1 tablespoon chopped mint

Fit processor with METAL BLADE. Process cucumber 5 seconds, until finely chopped. Remove to serving bowl. Process tomato 3 seconds. Add to bowl. Gently mix yogurt, cumin and pepper with vegetables. Before serving, sprinkle with mint. Makes 6 servings.

e

GAZPACHO-FILLED AVOCADOS

*Surround with deviled eggs and cucumber slices for a
light lunch.*

½ medium green pepper,
  seeded, cut in 1-inch pieces
½ small red onion, cut in
  ½-inch slices
1 clove garlic
½ cucumber, peeled, seeded
  and cut in chunks
1 large tomato, peeled
½ cup cold water
1 envelope unflavored gelatin

1 cup tomato juice
1 envelope (.19 ounce) or 2
  teaspoons instant beef-broth
  mix
3 tablespoons vinegar
1 teaspoon paprika
½ teaspoon each salt and basil
Dash of hot pepper sauce
1 tablespoon oil
3 large avocados, halved

Fit processor with METAL BLADE. Process pepper 3 seconds. Remove to large bowl.
Process onion and garlic 3 seconds. Combine with pepper. Process cucumber 3 seconds.
Remove to bowl. Process tomato 2 seconds. Remove to bowl. Add cold water to processor. Sprinkle gelatin over water. Heat tomato juice. Sprinkle broth mix over gelatin.
Process 2 seconds. With motor running, add heated tomato juice, vinegar, paprika, salt,
basil, hot pepper sauce and oil. Turn into bowl and chill until consistency of unbeaten
egg whites. Fold in chopped vegetables. Spoon into cavities of halved avocados, mound-
ing up. Serve any leftover mixture as garnish. Makes 6 servings.

LAYERED SUMMER SALAD

You may vary the vegetables to suit your garden.

4 ounces cheddar cheese
1 head romaine lettuce
1 large cucumber
1 cup elbow macaroni, cooked
  (2 cups)
8 ounces salami or pepperoni,
  chilled

1 medium red onion, peeled
½ pound green beans, trimmed,
  cut in 1-inch pieces and
  blanched
1 cup each mayonnaise and
  yogurt
1 teaspoon lemon juice
2 teaspoons caraway seed

Fit processor with SHREDDING DISC. Shred cheese. Remove. Fit processor with
SLICING DISC. Cut romaine leaves in lengths to stand in feed tube. Shred romaine.

Remove to bottom of large salad bowl. Slice cucumber. Spread over romaine. Spread macaroni over cucumber. Slice salami. Spread over macaroni. Slice onion. Spread over salami. Cover with green beans. Mix mayonnaise, yogurt, lemon juice and caraway seed. Pour evenly over salad. Sprinkle with cheese. Cover and refrigerate several hours or overnight. Toss just before serving. Makes 4 main-dish servings.

MARINATED MUSHROOM SALAD

A delicious salad that used to take much longer to prepare when we had to slice the mushrooms by hand.

½ cup parsley, stems removed
1 pound mushrooms
1 large green onion, white part only
1 small clove garlic

1 tablespoon prepared mustard
½ teaspoon salt
Freshly ground pepper
½ cup oil

Fit processor with METAL BLADE. Process parsley 5 seconds. Remove. Fit processor with SLICING DISC. Place mushrooms on their sides in feed tube. Slice, with gentle pressure. Turn into bowl. Fit processor with METAL BLADE. Combine onion, garlic, mustard, salt and pepper in processor. Process 3 seconds. With motor running, add oil very slowly through feed tube. Mixture should be consistency of mayonnaise. Toss mushrooms in sauce. Sprinkle with parsley before serving. Makes 4 servings.

MARGARET'S POTATO SALAD

Margaret always offers this special salad as her contribution to the Fourth of July picnic celebration.

5 medium all-purpose potatoes
½ cup parsley, stems removed
1 hardcooked egg
1½ pounds smoked sausage, such as kielbasa, cut in ½-inch pieces
2 medium stalks celery, cut in 1-inch lengths
1 medium onion, quartered

2 tablespoons bacon fat
1 tablespoon flour
1 cup chicken bouillon
2 tablespoons vinegar
1 teaspoon sugar
1 teaspoon mustard
Salt to taste
Freshly ground pepper

Cook potatoes, peel and dice while warm. Fit processor with METAL BLADE. Process parsley 3 seconds. Remove to small bowl. Process egg 2 seconds. Combine with parsley. Process sausage, half a pound at a time, for 3 seconds. It should be coarsely chopped. Remove to bowl with potatoes. Process celery 3 seconds, until coarsely chopped. Combine with potatoes and toss gently to mix. Process onion 2 seconds. Heat bacon fat in skillet and add onion. Cook over medium heat for 5 minutes. Sprinkle flour over onion. Stir until well blended. Pour in bouillon. Cook until smooth. Stir in vinegar, sugar, mustard, salt and pepper. Bring to a boil and pour over potato mixture, tossing well. Serve warm if possible, or, if cold, do not chill. Makes 4 to 5 servings.

TABBOULI

A healthy, tasty salad that combines the best of summer. Try it with leftover bits of poultry, fish or meat mixed in.

1 teaspoon salt
1¼ cups water
1 cup buckwheat groats (wheat pilaf)
½ cup mint leaves, packed
4 cups parsley, stems removed
5 green onions, white part only

1 large, ripe tomato, peeled and quartered
½ cup oil
¼ cup lemon juice
Salt to taste
Freshly ground pepper

Bring salt and water to a boil. Remove from heat and stir in groats. Cover pan and let stand for 30 minutes, until water has been absorbed. Turn into large bowl. Fit processor with METAL BLADE. Process mint leaves and half of parsley 10 seconds, until finely chopped. Stir into groats. Repeat with remainder of parsley. Add white part of scallions and tomato quarters to processor. Process 3 seconds. Stir into groats. Stir in oil, lemon juice, salt and pepper. Let stand 2 to 3 hours at room temperature before serving on greens. Makes 6 servings.

GERMAN-STYLE VEGETABLE SALAD PLATTER

*Also delicious served on greens with ham rolls and
hardcooked egg slices.*

Vinaigrette Dressing (recipe
  follows)
¼ medium head of green
  cabbage, cut in thin wedges
¼ medium head of red cabbage,
  cut in thin wedges
2 medium-size white turnips,
  peeled
2 small cucumbers, peeled
½ pound green beans, cooked
  and drained (about 2 cups; see
  Note)

1 medium onion, cut in
  quarters
2 pounds hot cooked potatoes,
  preferably new
1 tablespoon vinegar, preferably
  white
Salt and freshly ground or white
  pepper
Minced parsley
Chopped hardcooked egg yolk

Prepare dressing; set aside. Fit processor with coarse SHREDDING DISC. Shred cabbage. Remove to separate bowls or plastic bags. Lay turnips horizontally in feed tube. Shred. Remove to bowl or bag. Fit processor with SLICING DISC. Slice cucumbers. Remove to bowl or bag. Put beans in bowl. Fit processor with METAL BLADE. Pulse onion 4 to 5 times, until minced. Add 2 tablespoons onion to beans. Pour ⅓ cup dressing over each vegetable; toss lightly (or tightly seal bags and turn several times to mix). Refrigerate 1 to 2 hours, tossing vegetables or turning bags once or twice. Meanwhile peel and slice hot potatoes into bowl. Add remaining onion and ⅓ cup dressing, the vinegar, salt and pepper to taste; toss gently. Let stand 5 to 10 minutes. Mound in center of platter. With slotted spoon remove marinating vegetables from bowls or bags and arrange in mounds around potato salad. Season to taste with salt and pepper. (Reserve any dressing left in bowls, refrigerate and use for future salads.) Sprinkle potato salad with parsley and other vegetables with egg yolk. This potato salad is best served slightly warm. Makes 6 servings. *NOTE:* Or use 1 16-ounce can whole green beans, drained, or 1 10-ounce package frozen beans, cooked and drained.

VINAIGRETTE DRESSING

In bowl or jar with tight-fitting lid, stir or shake well 1 tablespoon sugar, 1 teaspoon salt, freshly ground or white pepper to taste and ⅓ cup each water and vinegar, preferably white. Add 1⅓ cups oil; beat or shake well. Shake before using. Makes 2 cups.

SANDWICHES AND SNACKS

Lunch, Picnic, Brown Bag, Portable, After-School

CORNED BEEF ON RYE

Hearty open-face sandwiches for a
quick lunch or supper.

4–6 slices rye bread
½ pound corned beef, cut in
   1-inch pieces
¼ cup mayonnaise

2 tablespoons prepared mustard
6 ounces Swiss cheese, cut in
   1-inch pieces
3 medium tomatoes, peeled and
   sliced

Fit processor with METAL BLADE. Toast bread slices on one side under broiler. Process corned beef 4 seconds. Add mayonnaise and mustard and process 4 seconds. Remove and spread over untoasted sides of bread slices. Process cheese 6 seconds, until grated. Sprinkle over corned beef mixture. Top with tomato slices. Place under broiler about 4 inches from heat. Broil until cheese is melted and bubbling. Serve with pickles. Makes 4 to 6 servings.

CROQUE MONSIEUR

An elegant French sandwich to serve with sliced
tomatoes and watercress.

8 ounces cheddar cheese cut in
   1-inch cubes
4 ounces ham, cut in 1-inch
   cubes
½ cup heavy cream

1 teaspoon prepared mustard
2 eggs
4 tablespoons butter or
   margarine
8–10 slices firm bread

Fit processor with METAL BLADE. Process cheese 6 seconds, until finely grated. Remove to bowl. Process ham 5 seconds. Add to cheese. Mix in cream and mustard, making a spreadable paste. Beat eggs lightly. Heat butter in large skillet. Spread cheese mixture on half of bread slices. Cover with remaining bread slices. Press together firmly. Dip sandwiches in beaten eggs, coating all sides. Sauté in butter until toasted and golden on both sides. Makes 4 servings. These can be made ahead, wrapped tightly in foil, and frozen. Reheat in 400° oven.

FRENCH PICNIC LOAF

Best when made 24 hours ahead. It travels well.

1 long loaf French bread
½ pound liverwurst, cut in
    1-inch pieces
3 green onions, including green
    tops, cut in 1-inch pieces
½ cup parsley, stems removed

2 hardcooked eggs
1 8-ounce package cream cheese
1 teaspoon Worcestershire sauce
¼ cup sherry
Salt to taste
Freshly ground pepper

Cut bread lengthwise and hollow out inside. Reserve crumbs for another use. Fit processor with METAL BLADE. Combine liverwurst and onions and process for 10 seconds. Add parsley. Process 5 seconds. Add eggs. Process 3 seconds. Add cream cheese, Worcestershire sauce and sherry. Process 6 seconds, until well blended. Add salt and pepper. Process 2 seconds. Fill loaf with mixture. Wrap in foil and refrigerate overnight. To serve: cut in thin slices. This can be frozen.

CHILI CHIPS

Special for snacks with cold drinks.

2 English muffins, frozen
3 tablespoons butter or
    margarine

½ teaspoon hot pepper flakes
¼ teaspoon ground cumin

Cut muffins in ¼-inch-thick vertical slices. Place on ungreased cookie sheet. Fit processor with METAL BLADE. Process remaining ingredients 8 to 10 seconds, until smooth. Spread lightly on both sides of muffin slices. Bake in preheated 450° oven 3 to 4 minutes on each side. Cool on racks. Makes 24.

PITA SCRAMBLE

Another take-along for a picnic supper. Just wrap in double foil.

2 large or 4 individual pita
    pocket breads
2 tablespoons butter or
    margarine
2 medium ribs celery, cut in
    1-inch lengths

1 medium apple, cored and
    quartered
4 eggs, lightly beaten
4 ounces Swiss cheese, cut in
    1-inch cubes
½ teaspoon prepared mustard

Split pita breads, opening up pocket. Fit processor with METAL BLADE. Put butter in large skillet over medium-low heat. Process celery 5 seconds, until finely chopped. Add to skillet. Process apple 3 seconds, until finely chopped. Add to celery. Sauté over medium heat until soft. Stir in eggs and cook, stirring, until almost set. Process cheese for 4 seconds. Add cheese and mustard to eggs and cook until firm. Fill pita pockets and serve immediately, or wrap in foil for a picnic. Makes 4 servings.

BAKED SAUSAGE ROLLS

These can be individually wrapped and frozen. Just bake and serve.

1 pound baloney, cut in 1-inch
    chunks
12 ounces Swiss or Monterey
    jack cheese, cut in 1-inch
    cubes
1 medium onion, sliced

8-ounce jar sweet pickles,
    drained and cut in ½-inch
    pieces
½ cup mayonnaise
1 tablespoon prepared mustard
10–12 hard rolls
Softened butter or margarine

Fit processor with METAL BLADE. Process baloney, half a pound at a time, for 8 seconds, until finely chopped. Remove to large bowl. Process cheese in two batches for 5 seconds. Remove to bowl with baloney. Process onion 4 seconds, until finely chopped. Remove to bowl. Process pickles 8 seconds, until finely chopped. Add to bowl. Add mayonnaise and mustard and mix all together. Split rolls and remove some of the inside. Butter and fill with baloney mixture. Press halves together and wrap each roll in foil. Bake in preheated 300° oven for 1 hour. These can be baked at home and taken to picnics. Makes 6 to 8 servings.

DESSERTS

Mousses, Frozen Desserts, Puddings

APPLE-BANANA CRUMBLE

A nice old-fashioned dessert.

4 large tart apples, peeled,
  cored and quartered
2 medium bananas
Juice of ½ lemon
1 large slice firm white or
  whole wheat bread

½ cup cranberries
½ cup walnuts
¾ cup brown sugar, packed
¼ cup butter or margarine
1 teaspoon cinnamon

Fit processor bowl with METAL SLICER. Place apple quarters in feed tube, rounded sides up. Slice apples. Peel bananas and slice. Empty processor bowl if necessary. Turn fruit into greased 1½-quart baking dish. Sprinkle with lemon juice. Fit processor bowl with METAL BLADE. Tear bread into pieces and add to bowl. Process 8 seconds until fine crumbs. Add remaining ingredients and process 10 seconds, until fruit and nuts are chopped and ingredients are well mixed. If necessary, pulse 2 to 3 times. Spread mixture over fruit. Bake in preheated 350° oven for 40 minutes, until topping is crisp and fruit is tender. Serve warm with ice cream or hard sauce. Makes 6 servings.

APPLE TART GRATINÉE

Pastry:

½ cup butter or margarine
1 cup flour

3 tablespoons confectioners'
sugar

Fit processor with METAL BLADE. Combine all ingredients in processor. Process 10 seconds, until mixture is crumbly. Turn out into 8-inch pie or tart pan. With palms of hands, push pastry over bottom and up sides of pan, forming shell. Chill at least 30 minutes. Place in preheated 425° oven and bake for 12 minutes, until lightly browned. Cool.

Filling:

8 medium tart apples, peeled,
cored and quartered
2 tablespoons brandy or 1
teaspoon vanilla
1 tablespoon butter or
margarine

½ teaspoon nutmeg
1 tablespoon grated lemon rind
⅓ cup sugar
2 ounces sharp cheddar or
Gruyere cheese

Fit processor with SLICING DISC. Place apple quarters, cut sides down, in feed tube and slice. Set aside 2 cups slices. Put remainder into saucepan. Cover and cook over medium-low heat until soft. Stir in brandy, butter, nutmeg, lemon rind and sugar. Cook, uncovered, until mixture is thick sauce. Cool. Chill. Fill tart shell with sauce. Arrange apple slices over top in circular pattern. Bake in preheated 375° oven 30 minutes. Fit processor with SHREDDING DISC. Shred cheese. Sprinkle cheese over tart and return to oven until cheese is melted. Serve warm. Makes 6 to 8 servings.

BANANA-RHUBARB COBBLER

*Top with softened vanilla ice cream
or banana yogurt.*

2 medium bananas
2 cups cut rhubarb
4 tablespoons sugar, divided
¼ teaspoon cinnamon
Dash of nutmeg
½ cup flour

1½ teaspoons baking powder
7 graham crackers, broken up
¼ cup margarine, cut in ½-inch
pieces
1 egg
¼ cup milk

Slice banana by hand. In greased shallow 1-quart baking dish, mix well bananas, rhubarb, 2 tablespoons sugar and spices. Combine ¼ cup flour with baking powder. Set aside. Fit processor with METAL BLADE. Process graham crackers with remaining flour 7 seconds, until crumbs are very fine. Add margarine. Process 4 seconds. Add egg and milk. Process 4 seconds. Add remaining ¼ cup flour. Pulse 4 or 5 times, just to mix. With spoon, drop evenly on fruit mixture. Sprinkle with remaining sugar. Bake in preheated 400° oven 25 to 30 minutes, or until pick inserted in center of topping comes out clean. Serve warm. Makes 4 generous servings.

ORANGE-BUTTER-RUM SAUCE

This sauce is good on plain fruit or ice cream.

1 unpeeled navel orange	½ cup sugar
5 tablespoons rum	¼ cup butter

Slice orange into 8 sections, removing white pith in center and blossom end. Fit processor with METAL BLADE. Process orange sections 10 seconds. Add rum and sugar. Process for 10 seconds, until there are no longer any large pieces of orange rind. Pour into saucepan and add butter. Heat until butter is melted and sauce is well blended. This sauce can be frozen. Makes about 1 cup.

CARROT COOKIES

These freeze.

2 cups flour	1 cup brown sugar, packed
1 teaspoon baking powder	3 eggs
½ teaspoon baking soda	⅓ cup undiluted orange juice
1 large carrot	concentrate
½ cup walnuts	1 teaspoon vanilla
½ cup shortening	½ teaspoon cinnamon
	1½ cups raisins

Combine ¼ cup flour with baking powder and baking soda. Set aside. Fit processor with SHREDDING DISC. Shred carrot. Remove. Fit processor with METAL BLADE. Process nuts 3 seconds. Remove. Combine shortening and sugar. Process 5 seconds. Add eggs, orange juice concentrate and vanilla. Process 3 seconds. Add 1¾ cups flour and cinnamon. Process 4 seconds. Add carrots, nuts and raisins. Process 3 seconds. Add flour mixture. Pulse 3 to 4 times. Drop by teaspoonfuls 2 inches apart on greased cookie sheet. Bake in preheated 350° oven 10 to 12 minutes, or until lightly browned around edges. Remove to rack; cool. Makes about 96.

CARROT-PERSIMMON SOUFFLÉ ROLL

*A nice combination of flavors and another
use for carrots.*

½ cup carrot, cut in chunks
4 eggs, separated
1¼ cups sugar
2 2-inch strips orange peel
1 teaspoon cinnamon
¾ cup flour
1 teaspoon baking powder

3 ripe persimmons
½ cup sugar
1 tablespoon lemon juice
1 tablespoon light corn syrup
1 cup heavy cream
¼ cup slivered almonds

Cook carrots until soft. Fit processor with METAL BLADE. Process carrots 5 seconds, until smooth. Remove and cool. Grease a 10 x 15-inch jellyroll pan. Line with waxed paper extending 1 inch over each end. Grease paper. Combine yolks, sugar, orange peel and cinnamon in processor. Process 10 seconds, until peel is chopped and mixture is smooth. Remove to bowl and stir in carrot purée. Combine flour and baking powder in sieve or sifter. Beat whites until stiff. Fold whites and flour mixture into yolk mixture. Spread batter in prepared pan. Bake in preheated 350° oven for 15 to 18 minutes. Turn out onto cloth. Remove pan. Let cake rest 5 minutes. Strip off paper. Roll up. Unroll and cool. Fit processor with METAL BLADE. Cut persimmons in half and scrape flesh into processor. Add sugar and lemon juice. Process 2 seconds, until smooth. Remove to bowl. Put ¼ cup persimmon purée into saucepan with corn syrup. Simmer until of spreadable consistency. Beat cream until stiff. Fold in remaining persimmon purée mixture. Spread over carrot roll. Roll up. Glaze with warm persimmon mixture. Sprinkle almonds down center of roll. It can be frozen. Makes 8 servings.

CHOCOLATE CREAM PUFFS WITH PEPPERMINT FILLING

An exciting finish to any meal, these puffs can be made ahead, filled and frozen.

Puffs:
½ cup butter or margarine
1 cup water
1 teaspoon sugar

2 tablespoons cocoa
¾ cup plus 2 tablespoons flour
4 large eggs

Combine butter, water and sugar in saucepan. Combine cocoa and flour in small bowl, stirring together. Fit processor with METAL BLADE. Bring butter and water to a full boil. Reduce heat to medium. Stir in flour mixture all at once, beating with spoon until dough is smooth and forms a ball, pulling away from the pan. Turn into processor. With motor running, add eggs through feed tube, one at a time. Process each egg 5 seconds. Drop dough onto lightly greased baking sheet by spoonfuls, making 8 puffs. Bake in preheated 375° oven for 45 minutes. Remove and prick with knife point. Return to oven for 5 minutes. Remove to rack to cool.

Filling:
1 quart vanilla ice cream, softened

1 cup peppermint hard candies (red and white striped)
Confectioners' sugar

Fit processor with METAL BLADE. Process candies 5 seconds, until broken into small pieces. Mix into ice cream. Cut tops off puffs and remove any uncooked dough inside. Fill with ice cream. Replace tops. Sprinkle with confectioners' sugar before serving. A pouring of chocolate sauce would really gild the lily. Filled puffs can be frozen. Makes 8 servings.

FROZEN CHRISTMAS PUDDING

This recipe can be halved for a small family, but it is nice to make something special for the holidays that will serve a larger group.

½ cup cider
1 cup raisins
2 slices whole wheat bread
1 teaspoon cinnamon
1 teaspoon nutmeg
½ teaspoon ginger
½ teaspoon allspice

1 cup walnuts, pecans or Brazil nuts
1½ cups mixed candied fruit and peel
½ gallon vanilla ice cream
1 lump of sugar
1 teaspoon lemon extract or rum

Fit processor with METAL BLADE. Heat cider. Add raisins and let stand 15 minutes. Drain. Break bread into pieces and add, with spices, to processor. Process 5 seconds. Spread crumbs on baking sheet and dry out in 350° oven for 10 to 15 minutes. Process nuts 3 seconds. Remove. Add 2 tablespoons bread crumbs to fruit and peel. Process in 3 batches (unless your bowl is oversized). Process 5 seconds until chopped. Soften ice cream. Mix in crumbs, nuts, fruit and raisins, blending well. Pack mixture into 2-quart pudding bowl. Freeze for 24 hours or longer. To serve: Remove from freezer and let stand at room temperature for 15 minutes. Run hot knife around edge of bowl and unmold onto serving platter. With a spoon, make an indentation in top of ice cream. Soak sugar lump in extract or rum and place in indentation. Decorate pudding with holly. At the table, light the sugar lump. Makes 8 to 10 servings.

CINNAMON BUTTER

½ cup butter
2 tablespoons granulated sugar

½ teaspoon cinnamon

Fit processor with METAL BLADE. Process all ingredients 10 seconds, or until well blended. Chill or freeze to use on French toast, pancakes, muffins or biscuits. Yield: ½ cup.

COFFEE-MAPLE NUT CUSTARD

*The "sauce" is on the bottom so don't think
the custard isn't done. Whipped cream makes
it extra special.*

¼ cup walnuts or pecans
2 tablespoons butter
1½ cups hot coffee

½ cup maple syrup
4 eggs, separated

Fit processor with METAL BLADE. Process nuts 3 seconds. Remove. Add butter to processor. With motor running, pour coffee through feed tube. Add maple syrup and egg yolks, one at a time, through feed tube. Stop motor. Add nuts. Pulse once. Beat whites of eggs until stiff. Pour coffee mixture over whites and fold together quickly. Turn into lightly greased 1½-quart baking dish. Set dish in pan of hot water. Bake in preheated 350° oven for 30 minutes. Remove from hot water and cool to lukewarm before serving. Makes 4 servings.

DATE-NUT TORTE

Rich, easy and delicious.

½ pound vanilla wafers
5 tablespoons frozen orange
  juice concentrate
1 cup raisins

1 cup pitted dates
1 cup walnuts or pecans
1 cup heavy cream

Fit processor with METAL BLADE. Process wafers for 10 seconds, until fine crumbs. Remove to bowl. Combine with orange juice concentrate, making a spreadable paste. Process raisins, dates and nuts together for 10 seconds, until mixture is well blended. Beat cream until stiff. Layer in 8-inch round dish: ½ wafers, ½ cream, ½ date mixture. Repeat. Freeze overnight. Unmold onto plate. Cut into wedges. Serve with lightly whipped cream. Makes 6 servings.

FRUIT-FILLED OVEN PANCAKE

*A wonderful dish for Sunday brunch, or dessert for a
soup-and-salad supper.*

¼ cup toasted almonds
1 medium banana
2 tart medium apples, cored,
    peeled and quartered
¼ cup butter or margarine
¾ cup milk

3 eggs
¾ cup flour
2 tablespoons sugar
½ teaspoon cinnamon
Confectioners' sugar
Sour cream or yogurt

Fit processor with METAL BLADE. Process almonds 2 seconds. Remove. Slice banana by hand. Fit processor with SLICING DISC. Slice apples. Heat butter in 10-inch oven-proof skillet. Add apples and banana to skillet. Sauté over medium heat until glazed and tender, about 5 minutes. Fit processor with METAL BLADE. Combine milk, eggs and flour and process 3 seconds. Sprinkle almonds, sugar and cinnamon over fruit slices. Pour egg mixture over fruit. Bake in preheated 425° oven for 20 to 25 minutes, until puffy and firm. Serve immediately with a sprinkle of confectioners' sugar and a dollop of sour cream or yogurt. Makes 4 brunch or 6 dessert servings.

FRESH FRUIT RING WITH CREAMY
LEMON SHERBET

*This sherbet can be served with the fruits of any
season for a refreshing, low-calorie dessert.*

1 large lemon
1 cup sugar
2 cups milk
6 large strawberries

3 kiwi fruits
2 medium bananas
3 medium peaches or nectarines

Fit processor with METAL BLADE. Cut lemon into quarters lengthwise. Remove any heavy white pith. Cut quarters in half across. Combine in processor with sugar. Process 20 seconds, or until there are no large pieces of skin remaining. Add milk and process 10 seconds. Pour into flat pan and place in freezer. When sherbet has frozen to the icy stage, scrape out and process 10 seconds, until smooth. Refreeze. Fit processor with SLICING DISC. Hull strawberries and place on sides in feed tube. Slice. Skin kiwi fruits and stand upright in feed tube. Slice. Slice bananas by hand. Peel, pit and quarter peaches. Place in feed tube, cut sides down. Slice. To serve: Place a scoop of sherbet in center of dessert plate. Surround with overlapping slices of fruits. Serve immediately. Makes 6 servings.

FROZEN COFFEE CREAM

¾ cup walnuts
1 envelope gelatin
½ cup sugar
½ cup hot coffee
6 ounces chocolate bits

2 cups milk, heated but not
　boiling
2 eggs
1 teaspoon vanilla
½ cup heavy cream

Fit processor with METAL BLADE. Process nuts 3 seconds. Remove. Combine gelatin and sugar, and process 1 second. With motor running, pour in hot coffee. Add chocolate bits. Process 3 seconds. Add milk. Process 2 seconds. Add eggs and vanilla. Process 2 seconds. Turn out into bowl and chill until syrupy. Whip cream until stiff. Fold cream and ½ cup nuts into coffee mixture. Turn into 1-quart serving dish. Freeze overnight. Before serving, sprinkle with remaining nuts. Makes 6 servings.

HOMEMADE MINCEMEAT

This makes a lot of mincemeat, but mincemeat is a wonderful gift, will keep indefinitely—with occasional stirring—and can go into pies, cookies, cakes, tarts and puddings.

1 pound beef shin
½ pound beef suet
6 large tart apples, cored and
　quartered
2 cups nuts
8 ounces mixed fruit peels
2 teaspoons salt
1 teaspoon cinnamon
1 tablespoon nutmeg

2 teaspoons allspice
2 teaspoons mace
1½ pounds brown sugar
2 cups raisins
2 cups currants
1 cup apricot or peach preserves
3 cups cider
1 cup rum or sherry
2 cups brandy

Place beef in water to cover. Bring to a boil. Reduce heat and simmer for 45 minutes, until tender. Remove and cool. Fit processor with SHREDDING DISC. Shred beef. Remove to large kettle. Shred beef suet and add to kettle. Shred apples. Add to kettle. Fit processor with KNIFE BLADE. Process nuts 5 seconds, one cup at a time. Add to kettle. Chop fruit peels and add with remaining ingredients. Bring to boil and cook over medium-low heat for 2 hours, or until mixture is thick. Stir occasionally. Turn into glass jars or crocks. Cover and store in refrigerator or cool place. Every 2 weeks, give mixture a stir and add 3 to 4 tablespoons rum or brandy. Makes approximately 3 quarts.

MUD PIES

Devastatingly rich but delicious.

1¼ cups flour	¼ cup milk
1 teaspoon baking powder	1 teaspoon vanilla
½ teaspoon baking soda	3 cups rolled oats
½ teaspoon salt	1 cup semisweet chocolate
1 cup butter or margarine	pieces
1 cup brown sugar, packed	1 pint butter-pecan ice cream
½ cup granulated sugar	2 cups butterscotch sauce
2 eggs	1 cup heavy cream, whipped

Combine flour, baking powder, soda and salt and set aside. Fit processor with METAL BLADE. Put butter and sugars into processor. Process 5 to 6 seconds, until blended. Add eggs and process 2 to 3 seconds. Add milk and vanilla and process 3 to 4 seconds, until well mixed. Add flour mixture and process 5 to 6 seconds. Add oats and process 2 to 3 seconds. Add chocolate bits and process 2 to 3 seconds. Turn mixture into bowl. Drop by tablespoonfuls onto lightly greased baking sheet, about 2 inches apart. Bake in preheated 350° oven for 12 minutes, until centers are no longer wet and soft. Remove to racks. When cool, make sandwiches of cookies, using ice cream as filling. Freeze. To serve: Pour warm butterscotch sauce over each "pie" and top with a spoonful of whipped cream. Makes 12 to 16 pies.

STUFFED PEAR AU CHOCOLAT

An elegant dessert that can be made ahead.

12 Bartlett pear halves
 (2 1-pound cans)
Rind of ½ orange
¼ cup sugar

8 ounces cream cheese
2 tablespoons frozen orange
 juice concentrate
Chocolate Sauce (recipe follows)

Drain pears and pat dry thoroughly. Fit processor with METAL BLADE. Combine orange rind and sugar. Process 15 seconds, until rind is finely chopped. Fit processor with PLASTIC BLADE. Add cream cheese and orange juice concentrate to processor. Process 5 seconds, until mixture is smooth. Put pear halves together with cheese mixture. Chill for several hours. Serve with Chocolate Sauce. Makes 6 servings.

CHOCOLATE SAUCE

1 cup heavy cream
2 tablespoons butter or
 margarine

6 ounces semisweet chocolate
 chips
1 teaspoon vanilla

Fit processor with METAL BLADE. Heat cream with butter. Put chocolate chips into processor. With motor running, add cream mixture. Process 20 seconds, or until smooth. Add vanilla. Process 1 second. Pour warm sauce over pears. Makes about 2 cups.

FROZEN PLUM CREAM

Cool and refreshing.

2 cups fresh plums, pitted and
 halved
¼ cup orange juice
2 tablespoons lemon juice

¾ cup sugar
2 cups milk
Spicy Plum Sauce (recipe
 follows)

Fit processor with METAL BLADE. Combine all ingredients except sauce. Process 15 seconds, until smooth. Turn mixture into ice cube trays or shallow pan. Freeze until outer edges are firm but center is still mushy. Return to processor. Process 10 seconds, until smooth. Turn into one-quart dish or mold. Freeze until firm. Serve from dish or turn out onto serving platter. Accompany with Spicy Plum Sauce. Makes 4 to 6 servings.

SPICY PLUM SAUCE

½ cup walnuts
1 pound fresh plums, pitted and sliced
1 cup sugar
1 stick cinnamon

5 whole cloves
1 tablespoon cornstarch
2 tablespoons lemon juice
2 tablespoons orange juice

Fit processor with METAL BLADE. Process walnuts 3 seconds. Remove. Combine plums and sugar in saucepan. Add cinnamon and cloves. Simmer gently until fruit is tender, about 15 minutes. Stir cornstarch into lemon and orange juices. Stir into plum sauce. Cook, stirring, until thickened. Turn into processor. Process 5 seconds. Combine with walnuts and serve warm over Frozen Plum Cream. Makes about 2 cups.

STRAWBERRY BUTTER CREAM

1 pint strawberries, hulled, halved
4 ounces cream cheese, cut in 1-inch pieces

4 tablespoons butter, cut in 1-inch pieces
½ cup confectioners' sugar

Fit processor with METAL BLADE. Process all ingredients 15 seconds, until smooth. Chill before spreading. This can be frozen and used on waffles, toast, English muffins.

BREADS AND PASTRIES

Breads, Cakes, Cookies, Pies

BANANA-NUT PANCAKES

Good for school-day breakfasts.

1 cup flour
1 teaspoon baking powder
¼ cup walnuts
1 medium banana, cut in
    1-inch pieces

1 cup milk
1 egg
2 tablespoons oil
2 tablespoons sugar
¼ teaspoon salt

Combine ¼ cup flour with baking powder and set aside. Fit processor with METAL BLADE. Process walnuts 3 seconds. Remove. Process banana 3 seconds. Add milk, egg and oil. Process 3 seconds. Add ¾ cup flour, sugar and salt. Process 2 seconds. Add flour, baking-powder mixture and nuts. Pulse 3 to 4 times. Drop by scant ¼ cupfuls onto hot, lightly greased griddle. Cook, turning once, until golden. Serve with margarine and syrup. Makes 12.

BRAN MUFFINS

A Monday morning treat to whip up in seconds.

1 cup flour
1 teaspoon baking powder
1 teaspoon baking soda
1 cup butter or margarine, cut
    in ½-inch slices

¼ cup brown sugar, packed
1 egg
1 cup bran flakes
½ teaspoon salt

Combine ¼ cup flour with baking powder and soda. Set aside. Combine butter and brown sugar. Process 5 seconds. Add egg. Process 10 seconds, until mixture is creamy. Add bran flakes and salt. Process 5 seconds. Add ¾ cup flour. Process 3 seconds. Add remaining flour and baking powder mixture. Pulse 4 or 5 times. Spoon into well-greased muffin tins. Bake in preheated 400° oven for 20 minutes. Turn out and serve warm. Makes 14 muffins.

PIZZA BREAD

Can be cooked on the grill along with the hamburgers.

2 cloves garlic, sliced
⅓ cup oil
1 large tomato, peeled, or 2
    canned plum tomatoes,
    drained

1 teaspoon oregano
8 ounce loaf (16 inches long)
    Italian bread, split
Salt and pepper to taste

Fit processor with METAL BLADE. Process garlic and oil 4 to 5 seconds, until well blended. Add tomato and oregano. Process 3 to 4 seconds. Spoon over cut sides of bread. Sprinkle with salt and pepper. Place halves together; wrap in foil. Bake in preheated 400° oven 10 minutes; open foil; separate halves, cut side up. Bake 5 minutes longer. Cut diagonally in 1-inch slices. *NOTE:* Or cook on grill 10 minutes, then unwrap and cook 5 minutes longer. Makes 32 pizzas.

CARROT-ORANGE LOAF

Slice thin and spread with cream cheese.

1 cup walnuts
2 large carrots
2 cups flour
1 teaspoon each baking powder
    and soda
Peel of 1 orange

1 cup brown sugar, packed
½ cup butter or margarine, cut
    in ½-inch pieces
2 eggs
½ teaspoon salt
½ teaspoon each allspice and
    nutmeg

Fit processor with METAL BLADE. Process walnuts 4 seconds. Remove. Fit processor with SHREDDING DISC. Cut carrots in lengths to fit feed tube vertically. Stand up in feed tube and shred. Remove. Combine ¼ cup flour with baking powder and soda. Set aside. Fit processor with METAL BLADE. Combine orange peel and sugar. Process 10 seconds, until peel is finely grated. Add butter and process 5 seconds. Add eggs. Process 3 seconds. Add 1¾ cups flour, salt and spices. Process 4 seconds. Add carrots and nuts. Process 3 seconds. Add remaining ¼ cup flour mixture. Pulse 3 to 4 times, until just mixed. Turn out into greased 8 x 5 x 3-inch loaf pan. Bake in preheated 325° oven 50 to 60 minutes, or until pick inserted in center comes out clean. Cool in pan 5 minutes; turn out to cool completely.

CHEESY BRIOCHE LOAF

This is a handsome, buttery loaf that makes wonderful sandwiches or a base for creamed chicken or eggs benedict. It can also be baked in a ring and filled with creamed mushrooms.

½ cup butter or margarine
1 package yeast
¼ cup lukewarm water
1 teaspoon sugar
2 ounces Fontina cheese, cut in
   1-inch cubes

2 ounces Parmesan cheese, cut
   in 1-inch cubes
3 eggs, 1 separated
2 cups flour
1 teaspoon salt
1 egg yolk beaten with 1
   tablespoon water

Melt butter and set aside to cool. Dissolve yeast in water with sugar and let stand until bubbly. Fit METAL BLADE into processor. Process cheeses for 10 seconds, until finely grated. Add eggs, flour and salt. Process 2 seconds. Add yeast. Process 1 second. With motor running, add butter through feed tube. Process 2 seconds, or until dough climbs up spindle. Feel dough. If it is buttery and no longer sticky, scrape out and place in greased bowl. If sticky, add about 2 tablespoons flour and process 5 seconds. Cover bowl and let stand in warm place until light and puffy. It will not be doubled. Punch down. Refrigerate, covered, for at least 4 hours. Divide into 3 parts. Roll each part into a "snake" 11 inches in length. Braid the 3 pieces of dough. Place in greased 8 x 5-inch loaf pan. Cover and let rise until puffy. Dough will be about 1 inch below top rim of pan. Brush with beaten yolk. Bake in 375° oven for 40 minutes. Turn out onto rack to cool. Makes 1 loaf.

CINNAMON-RAISIN TOASTING BREAD

This is better than any bakery loaf and wonderful for breakfast, lunch or tea.

1 package yeast
¼ cup lukewarm water
1 cup milk
¾ cup sugar
1 teaspoon cinnamon

5 tablespoons melted butter or
   margarine
2 cups unbleached flour
1½ cups whole wheat flour
1 teaspoon salt
½ cup raisins

Dissolve yeast in water and let stand until bubbly. Heat milk to lukewarm. Combine ¼ cup sugar with cinnamon. Set aside. Fit processor with METAL BLADE. Add milk, remaining ½ cup sugar and 4 tablespoons melted butter to processor. Process 1 second. Add yeast. Process 2 seconds. Add unbleached flour. Process 3 seconds. Add whole wheat flour. Process 15 to 20 seconds. Add salt. If motor falters or will not move dough around bowl, add more flour, 2 tablespoons at a time, until processor starts again. Test dough with fingers and, if no longer sticky, remove to floured board. Knead in raisins. Turn into greased bowl. Cover. Let rise in warm place until doubled in bulk. Punch down. Shape into loaf. Place in greased 8 x 5-inch loaf pan. Cover. Let rise in warm place until doubled or loaf has risen to top of pan. Bake in 350° oven for 40 minutes. Turn out onto rack. Brush with remaining tablespoon melted butter and sprinkle all over with sugar-cinnamon mixture. Cool before slicing. This makes very good French toast when sliced 1 inch thick. Makes 1 loaf.

BUTTERMILK COFFEE CAKE

This easy coffee cake has everything—it looks pretty, tastes good and freezes well.

½ cup walnuts or pecans
¼ cup brown sugar, packed
1 teaspoon cinnamon
2 cups flour
1 teaspoon baking powder
1 teaspoon baking soda
½ cup butter or margarine, cut in ½-inch slices

1 cup sugar
2 eggs
1 cup buttermilk
½ teaspoon vanilla
1 teaspoon salt
3 tablespoons dark corn syrup

Fit processor with METAL BLADE. Combine nuts, brown sugar and cinnamon. Pulse 3 to 4 times, until chopped and well mixed. Remove. Combine ¼ cup flour, baking powder and baking soda. Set aside. Combine butter and sugar. Process 3 seconds. Add eggs. Process 2 seconds. Add buttermilk and vanilla. Process 2 seconds. Add 1¾ cups flour and salt. Process 5 seconds, until mixed. Scrape down sides with spatula. Add remaining flour and baking-soda mixture. Pulse 3 to 4 times. Grease a 1½-quart tube pan. Pour corn syrup over bottom. Sprinkle with half of nut mixture. Spread half of batter over nuts. Sprinkle with remaining nuts. Add remaining batter. Bake in preheated 350° oven for 45 minutes, or until cake tests done. Turn out onto rack to cool. Scrape out any nut mixture remaining in pan and spread over cake. Makes 1 tube cake.

DATE-NUT COFFEE RING

Filling:

1 8-ounce package pitted dates

¼ cup walnuts

½ cup each sugar and hot water

2 teaspoons lemon juice

Fit processor with METAL BLADE. Process dates 8 seconds, until chopped. Add nuts. Process 4 seconds. Combine in saucepan with sugar, water and lemon juice. Cook over medium heat, stirring frequently, until thickened and bubbly. Cool.

Dough:

2 cups flour

1 tablespoon baking powder

¾ teaspoon salt

¼ teaspoon mace

2 tablespoons sugar

6 tablespoons butter or margarine, cut in ½-inch pieces

1 egg

½ cup milk

Combine ¼ cup flour with baking powder and set aside. Combine remaining flour, salt, mace, sugar and butter in processor. Process 6 to 7 seconds. In measuring cup, slightly beat egg; add enough milk to make ¾ cup. Add to flour mixture. Process 5 seconds. Add ¼ cup flour and baking-powder mixture and pulse 3 to 4 times, just to blend. Turn out on lightly floured surface and knead gently about 30 seconds. On lightly floured waxed paper, roll dough to 12 x 9-inch rectangle. Spread with filling almost to edges. Starting at long side, roll as for jellyroll. Pinch seam to seal. Place seam side down on lightly greased baking sheet; join ends to shape into ring. Pinch ends together to seal. With kitchen shears, cut through ring at 1-inch intervals to about 1 inch from center. Turn each slice slightly on its side. Bake in preheated 400° oven about 20 minutes, or until evenly browned.

Icing:

½ cup confectioners' sugar

1 tablespoon milk

½ teaspoon vanilla

In small bowl, stir all ingredients well. Drizzle on warm coffee ring. Serve warm. Makes 8 servings.

CRANBERRY-NUT BREAD

*Try it warm and toasted with cream cheese
for breakfast.*

1 cup fresh cranberries
1 cup walnuts
Rind of 1 orange, in strips
1 cup sugar
2 cups flour
½ teaspoon salt

1½ teaspoons baking powder
½ teaspoon baking soda
1 egg
2 tablespoons oil
¾ cup orange juice

Fit processor with METAL BLADE. Process cranberries 6 seconds, until finely chopped. Remove to large bowl. Process nuts 2 to 3 seconds. Combine with cranberries. Add orange rind to processor with sugar. Process 10 seconds, until rind is finely chopped. Combine ½ cup flour with salt, baking powder and soda. Set aside. Add egg to processor. Process 1 second. Add oil. Process 1 second. Add orange juice. Process 1 second. Add 1½ cups flour. Process 3 to 4 seconds, until well mixed in. Add ½ cup flour mixture. Pulse 3 or 4 times. Flecks of flour will show and mixture will be bubbly. Turn out and combine with cranberries and nuts. Fold together. Turn into well-greased 8 x 5-inch loaf pan. Bake in 350° oven for 1 hour and 10 minutes. Turn out onto rack. Cool before slicing. Makes 1 loaf.

HAM-AND-CHEESE BISCUITS

2 cups flour
4 teaspoons baking powder
1 teaspoon salt
2 ounces ham, cut in 1-inch
  cubes
4 ounces sharp cheese, cut in
  1-inch cubes

6 tablespoons butter or
  margarine, cut in ½-inch
  pieces
½ teaspoon prepared mustard
1 egg
⅓ cup milk

Combine ½ cup flour with baking powder and salt. Set aside. Fit processor with METAL BLADE. Process ham 3 seconds. Remove to bowl. Process cheese 3 seconds. Combine with ham. Add butter to processor with remaining flour. Process 3 seconds. Add mustard and egg. Process 2 seconds. Add milk. Process 2 seconds. Add remaining ½ cup flour and baking-powder mixture. Pulse 3 times. Turn out onto floured board and knead twice. Roll out to ¼-inch thickness. Cut into 2½-inch rounds. Put one teaspoon ham-and-cheese mixture on each round. Top with another round and pinch edges together. Set biscuits on greased baking sheet. Bake in 400° oven for 15 minutes, until risen and golden. Serve hot. These freeze well. Makes approximately 2 dozen.

HERBED PORTUGUESE BREAD

Great to take along on a picnic.

1 green onion, cut in ½-inch
  lengths, green top included
2 tablespoons parsley, stems
  removed
1 tablespoon snipped dill weed
½ cup boiling water

1 teaspoon salt
4 tablespoons solid vegetable
  shortening
¼ cup lukewarm water
1 package yeast
3–4 cups flour

Fit processor with METAL BLADE. Process onion, parsley and dill 6 seconds. Add boiling water, salt and shortening to processor. Process 1 second. Let stand until luke-warm. Dissolve yeast in ¼ cup water. Add to processor. Let stand 5 minutes. Process 1 second. Add 3 cups flour. Process 20 seconds. Add ½ cup flour. Process until dough forms a ball around spindle. If dough is still sticky, add a bit more flour. When dough is smooth and elastic, turn out and knead briefly. Turn into greased bowl and cover. Let stand in warm place until doubled. Punch down. Fit into greased 9-inch round baking pan. Cover and let stand until dough is doubled in bulk. Bake in preheated 400° oven for 45 minutes, or until done. Brush top with melted shortening and cool on rack. Makes 1 9-inch loaf.

ORANGE-WALNUT ROLLS

1 cup orange juice
4 tablespoons shortening
1 package yeast
1 egg
6 tablespoons brown sugar,
  packed

½ teaspoon salt
3–4 cups unbleached flour
Filling (recipe follows)
Icing (recipe follows)

Heat orange juice with shortening until shortening is melted. Fit processor with METAL BLADE. Pour orange juice mixture into processor and let stand until lukewarm. Sprinkle yeast over orange juice and let stand 5 minutes. Process 1 second. Add egg, sugar and salt. Process 2 seconds. Add 3 cups flour. Process 20 seconds. Add remaining flour gradually, ½ cup at a time, processing until dough forms a ball around spindle. Dough should be soft but not sticky. Turn out and knead briefly. Place in greased bowl. Cover and let stand in warm place until double in bulk. Roll out on floured board to 12 x 18-inch rectangle. Spead with filling. Roll up as for jelly roll. Cut in 1-inch slices. Place close together in greased 9 x 12-inch pan. Cover and let stand until puffy and light. (The dough will not be doubled.) Bake in preheated 375° oven for 25 to 30 minutes. Spread with icing while warm. Makes approximately 20 rolls.

FILLING

Rind of 1 orange
½ cup brown sugar, packed
½ teaspoon ground nutmeg

½ cup walnuts
2 tablespoons softened butter or
  margarine

Fit processor with METAL BLADE. Remove orange rind in strips with vegetable peeler. Place in processor with sugar, nutmeg and walnuts. Process 15 seconds, until finely grated. Spread rectangle of dough with butter and cover with orange mixture.

ICING

1 cup confectioners' sugar
2–3 tablespoons milk

1 teaspoon vanilla

Fit processor with METAL BLADE. Combine all ingredients and process 5 seconds, adding more liquid if necessary to make icing of spreadable consistency.

PESTO BREAD

Good with any kind of pasta.

½ cup oil, preferably olive
⅓ cup loosely packed parsley
⅓ cup fresh basil leaves
4 medium garlic cloves

¼ teaspoon salt
Freshly ground pepper
8-ounce loaf (16 inches long)
French bread, split

Fit processor with METAL BLADE. Place all ingredients except bread in processor. Process 10 seconds, or until smooth. Push down from sides with spatula if necessary. Spread mixture over cut sides of bread. Place halves together. Wrap in foil. Bake in preheated 400° oven 10 minutes. Open foil. Separate halves, cut sides up. Bake 5 minutes longer. Cut in 1-inch slices. This can be prepared ahead, wrapped and frozen. Bake from frozen state, allowing 30 minutes.

GREEN-ONION LOAF

Serve with soup and salad.

1 ounce Parmesan or Romano
   cheese, cut in ½-inch cubes
3 green onions, cut in ½-inch
   lengths

½ cup butter or margarine, cut
   in tablespoons
Freshly ground pepper to taste
8-ounce loaf (16 inches long)
French bread, split

Fit processor with METAL BLADE. Process cheese 5 to 6 seconds. Add onions, process 4 to 5 seconds. Add butter. Process 8 to 10 seconds, until mixture is smooth. Add pepper. Process 1 second. Spread on cut surfaces of bread. Place halves together; wrap in foil. Bake in preheated 400° oven 10 minutes; open foil; separate halves, cut side up. Bake 5 to 7 minutes longer, or until bubbly and lightly browned around edges. Cut in 1-inch slices. Makes 32.

RAISIN-CHEESE BREAD

1 cup milk
4 ounces sharp cheddar cheese,
  cut in 1-inch cubes
1 tablespoon sugar
1 tablespoon butter or
  margarine

1½ teaspoons salt
1 package active yeast
¼ cup warm water
2¾–3 cups flour
1 cup raisins

Scald milk. Fit processor with METAL BLADE. Process cheese 3 seconds. Add sugar, butter, salt and milk to cheese. Process 2 seconds. Let stand until lukewarm. Dissolve yeast in warm water. Let stand until bubbly. Add to processor. Process 1 second. Add 2 cups flour. Process 10 seconds. Add raisins and ½ cup flour. Process 8 seconds, or until dough forms a ball around spindle. If dough is still sticky, add a little more flour and process until smooth. Turn out into greased bowl. Cover and let stand in warm place until doubled. Punch down. Shape into loaf and put in greased 9 x 5 x 3-inch loaf pan. Cover and let rise until doubled. Bake in preheated 375° oven for 40 to 45 minutes. Turn out on rack and cool before cutting. Makes especially good sandwiches, toasted.

SALLY LUNN

A non-sweet bread to serve warm
with butter and jam.

2 packages yeast
1 tablespoon sugar
¼ cup lukewarm water
2 cups milk
4 cups flour

4 tablespoons melted butter or
  margarine
2 eggs
1 teaspoon salt

Fit processor with METAL BLADE. Sprinkle yeast and sugar in bowl of processor. Add water. Process 1 second. Let stand for 5 minutes. Meanwhile, heat milk to lukewarm. Add milk to processor with 2 cups flour. Process 5 seconds. Add butter, eggs, remaining flour and salt. Process until dough forms a ball around spindle and is smooth and shiny. Turn into well-greased and floured Bundt pan. Cover and let rise in warm place until light and doubled in bulk. Bake in 400° oven for 30 minutes. Turn out onto rack and cool. This is very good toasted.

WHEAT LOAF

This is a nice bread to take along on picnics.

1 package yeast
1¼ cups lukewarm water
2 tablespoons shortening
¼ cup molasses
1 teaspoon instant coffee
   powder

1 teaspoon salt
1 cup whole wheat flour
1½ cups unbleached flour
¼ cup toasted wheat germ

Soak yeast in ¼ cup water. Fit processor with METAL BLADE. Combine remaining water, shortening, molasses, coffee and salt in processor. Process 2 seconds. When yeast is bubbly, add, and process 1 second. Add whole wheat and unbleached flours. Process 10 seconds. Add wheat germ. Process until dough climbs spindle. Stop processor. Remove cover, and if dough is sticky to the touch, add ¼ cup additional unbleached flour and process 10 seconds, or until smooth. Turn out into greased bowl. Cover and let rise in warm place until doubled. Turn out and punch down. Shape into round loaf to fit into greased 8-inch round cake pan. With sharp knife point, score top in cuts ¼ inch deep to make a diamond pattern (as for ham). Cover and let rise until dough reaches top of pan. Bake in 375° oven for 30 minutes. Turn out and cool on rack. Makes 1 8-inch loaf.

RICH WHITE BREAD

1 package yeast
½ cup lukewarm water
1 cup sour cream
1 egg

2 tablespoons oil
3¼ cups flour, approximately
1 teaspoon salt

Add yeast to water and let stand until bubbly. Fit processor with METAL BLADE. Combine sour cream, egg and oil and process 2 seconds. Add yeast. Process 1 second. Add 3 cups flour and salt. Process 20 seconds, or until dough forms a ball. If blade spins without moving dough, add more flour. Dough should be smooth but not sticky. Turn out onto floured board and knead for 1 minute. Turn into greased bowl and cover. Let rise in warm place until doubled in bulk. Punch down. Let rise a second time until doubled. Punch down. Shape into loaf and place in greased 8 x 5-inch loaf pan. Cover and let rise until doubled. Bake at 375° for 40 minutes. Cool on rack. This bread is good for both sandwiches and toast. Makes 1 loaf.

ONION ROLLS

*Give a lift to that hamburger, or serve these
on the side.*

¼ medium onion
¼ cup butter or margarine, cut
   in tablespoons

6 hamburger buns

Fit processor with METAL BLADE. Process onion 3 to 4 seconds. Add butter. Process 7 to 8 seconds, until smooth. Place buns, top side up, in 13 x 9 x 2-inch baking pan. Spread onion mixture evenly over tops. Bake in preheated 375° oven 5 to 7 minutes, or until lightly browned. Serve hot. Makes 6.

APPLE KUCHEN

*This makes a small cake, just right for
a small family.*

1 medium-size apple, cored,
   peeled and quartered
½ teaspoon salt
1 teaspoon baking powder
1¼ cups flour
½ cup butter or margarine, cut
   in pieces

¼ cup sugar
1 egg
1 teaspoon vanilla
2 tablespoons Cinnamon Butter
   (recipe on page 119)

Fit processor with SLICING DISC. Place apple quarters, cut side down, in feed tube and slice. Remove. Fit processor with METAL BLADE. Add salt and baking powder to ¼ cup flour and set aside. Put butter and sugar into processor and process 5 to 6 seconds, until smooth. Add egg. Process 2 seconds. Add vanilla. Process 1 second. Add 1 cup flour. Process 3 seconds. Add ¼ cup flour and baking powder mixture. Pulse 3 to 4 times. Turn out into greased 8-inch round pan. Arrange apple slices in circles over top. Dot with Cinnamon Butter. Bake in 350° oven for 45 to 50 minutes. Serve warm with whipped cream or ice cream. Makes 4 to 5 servings.

SPICY APPLE CAKE

A good cake for a party. It freezes well, serves a lot of people and nobody can refuse it.

1 cup walnuts or pecans
½ cup raisins
3 medium apples, peeled, cored, cut into 1-inch chunks
3 eggs
1 cup oil
1 cup granulated sugar

1 cup brown sugar, packed
2 cups flour
1 teaspoon baking soda
1 teaspoon vanilla
1 teaspoon cinnamon
½ teaspoon nutmeg
½ teaspoon salt

Fit processor with METAL BLADE. Put nuts and raisins into processor. Process 4 seconds. Remove to large bowl. Process apples 3 seconds, or until coarsely chopped. Remove to bowl with nuts. Add eggs and oil to processor. Process 1 second. Combine ½ cup flour with baking soda and set aside. Add sugars to processor. Process 2 seconds. Add remaining 1½ cups flour, vanilla, spices and salt. Process 4 seconds. Add ½ cup flour mixture. Pulse 3 times. Turn into bowl with apple mixture and fold together. Turn into well-greased and floured Bundt pan. Bake in preheated 350° oven 1 hour. Turn out onto rack. Serve warm with chilled whipped cream, or sprinkle with powdered sugar.

APRICOT ALMOND CAKE

Delicious for a party dessert, and pretty too.

1½ cups apricot preserves
2 tablespoons frozen orange juice concentrate
2 cups flour
1 teaspoon baking powder
1 teaspoon baking soda
¼ teaspoon salt

1 8-ounce package cream cheese
½ cup butter or margarine
1 cup sugar
2 eggs
½ teaspoon almond extract
¼ cup milk
¼ cup toasted slivered almonds

Fit processor with METAL BLADE. Combine apricot preserves and orange juice concentrate and process 2 seconds. Remove. Combine flour, baking powder, soda and salt. Set aside. Without washing bowl, process cream cheese, butter and sugar 9 seconds. Add eggs, milk and almond extract. Process 5 seconds. Add dry ingredients. Pulse 6 times. Scrape down sides. Pulse 4 times. If a little flour still shows, don't worry. Spread half the mixture in a greased and floured 9-inch spring-form pan. Cover with 1 cup apricot mixture. Cover with remaining batter. Bake for 45 to 50 minutes, in a 350° oven until cake tests done. Place pan on rack until room temperature. Remove cake from pan. Spread top and sides with remaining apricot mixture. Sprinkle almonds over top, cluster in center or make a ring around edge. This cake will freeze. Makes 8 to 10 servings.

APRICOT MOUSSE CAKE

A light, fruit-filled dessert that can be done way ahead.

3 slices white bread, torn in
    pieces
¼ cup sugar
1 1-pound can apricots
1 envelope unflavored gelatin
½ teaspoon almond extract

1 teaspoon vanilla
1½ cups heavy or whipping
    cream
2 tablespoons grated orange rind
4 tablespoons slivered almonds

Rinse out a 1-quart mold with cold water. Do not dry. Place in freezer. Fit processor with METAL BLADE. Add bread and sugar. Process 5 seconds. Remove to small bowl. Drain apricots, reserving ¼ cup juice. Dissolve gelatin in juice over low heat. Pit apricots if necessary. Place apricots in processor with flavorings. Process 2 seconds, until puréed. Add dissolved gelatin to processor. Process 1 second. Beat cream until stiff. Fold apricot mixture into cream. Remove mold from freezer. Turn ⅓ of apricot mixture into mold. Cover with half of bread crumbs. Repeat until both mixtures are used up. Cover and freeze overnight. To unmold: dip mold into hot water for 10 seconds and turn out onto serving platter. Garnish with grated orange rind and slivered almonds. Makes 6 servings.

BABA AU RHUM

A formerly formidable dessert that is now easier than pie.

1 package dry yeast
⅓ cup lukewarm milk
4 eggs
¼ cup sugar
½ teaspoon salt
½ cup melted butter or
   margarine

3 cups unbleached flour
¼ cup rum
2 tablespoons butter
½ cup brown sugar, packed
⅓ cup orange juice

Dissolve yeast in milk and let stand 5 minutes, until bubbly. Fit processor with METAL BLADE. Add eggs, sugar, salt and butter to processor. Process 5 seconds. Add yeast and pulse twice. Add flour and process 10 seconds, until well blended. If necessary, remove top and scrape down sides with spatula. Dough should be soft. Scrape into greased bowl and cover. Let stand in warm place until doubled in bulk (approximately 1 hour). Dough will be light and springy. Punch down and turn into well-greased 8-inch tube or Bundt pan. Cover, and let rise in warm place until doubled in bulk. Bake in preheated 350° oven for 40 minutes. If top is quite brown after 20 minutes, cover loosely with foil. Meanwhile, combine in saucepan the rum, butter, sugar and orange juice. Bring to a boil. Reduce heat and simmer for 10 minutes. Keep warm over very low heat. Turn baba out onto rack. With skewer or ice pick, make holes all over upturned side. Spoon rum sauce over baba, letting it soak in. When cooked, slice and serve with Custard Sauce (see page 143 for recipe). Makes 8 to 10 servings. Leftover baba makes wonderful French toast.

DESSERT FINGERS

Nice to serve with fresh fruit or ice cream.

18 thin slices firm-textured
   white bread (1-pound loaf)
6 tablespoons butter or
   margarine

¼ cup brandy or fruit-flavored
   liqueur
6 tablespoons fruit preserves
Confectioners' sugar

Trim crust from bread (use crusts and heels to make crumbs). Fit processor with METAL BLADE. Combine butter, liqueur and preserves. Process 9 to 10 seconds, until well blended and smooth. Spread each slice with mixture. Bake on ungreased cookie sheet in preheated 400° oven 7 minutes, or until lightly browned around edges. Cool on rack. Stack slices to make 6 stacks of 3 slices each. Dust with confectioners' sugar. Cut each stack in thirds lengthwise. Makes 18.

CUSTARD SAUCE

4 egg yolks
1 teaspoon flour
½ cup sugar

1½ cups milk
1 teaspoon vanilla

Fit processor with METAL BLADE. Combine yolks, flour and sugar. Process 3 seconds. Heat milk to scalding. With motor running, pour hot milk through feed tube. Turn mixture back into saucepan and cook, stirring, over medium heat for 4 to 5 minutes until sauce has thickened and coats back of spoon. Turn into bowl and cover with plastic wrap. When cool, stir in vanilla. Makes 2 cups.

BRANDIED CHOCOLATE POUND CAKE

Keep in the freezer for emergency teatime rations.

1½ cups flour
1 teaspoon baking powder
½ cup cocoa
½ teaspoon salt
2 cups butter or margarine, cut
    into ½-inch pieces

4 eggs
1½ cups sugar
1 teaspoon vanilla
2 tablespoons brandy

Combine ¼ cup flour with baking powder. Set aside. Fit processor with METAL BLADE. Combine 1 cup flour, cocoa, salt and butter in processor. Process 10 seconds, until smooth. Add eggs and process 5 seconds. Add sugar, vanilla and brandy. Process 3 seconds. Add remaining ¼ cup flour. Pulse 3 times. Turn into well-greased and floured 8 x 5-inch loaf pan. Place in cold oven. Set temperature for 350° and bake for 1 hour, or until cake tests done. Cool in pan for 15 minutes. Turn out onto rack. Do not slice for 24 hours. Serves 8 to 10.

BROWN SUGAR-NUT CAKE

So easy a child could, and should, do it.

2 cups flour	1 cup brown sugar, packed
1 teaspoon baking soda	1 egg
¾ teaspoon baking powder	1 cup buttermilk
1 cup walnuts or pecans	1 teaspoon vanilla

Fit processor with METAL BLADE. Combine ¼ cup flour with soda and baking powder and set aside. Process nuts 5 seconds, until finely chopped. Remove. Combine sugar and egg. Process 5 seconds, until smooth. Add buttermilk and vanilla. Process 2 seconds. Add flour. Process 4 seconds. Add nuts and remaining flour mixture. Pulse 3 to 4 times, until just blended. Turn into greased 9 x 9-inch baking pan. Bake in preheated 350° oven for 30 to 40 minutes, until cake tests done. Serve warm with whipped cream. Makes 6 servings.

CRANBERRY UPSIDE-DOWN CAKE

A good cake for the holidays that freezes well.

2 cups cranberries, washed	2 teaspoons baking powder
½ cup almonds	¼ teaspoon salt
6 tablespoons butter or	2 2-inch strips orange peel
margarine	1 egg
1½ cups sugar	½ cup buttermilk
1¼ cups flour	½ teaspoon almond extract

Fit processor with METAL BLADE. Chop cranberries by pulsing 10 times. Add almonds and pulse 3 to 4 times. Heat 2 tablespoons butter in 8-inch round cake pan or ovenproof skillet over medium heat. Add 1 cup sugar. When butter has melted, stir in cranberry mixture. Simmer 5 minutes. Meanwhile, combine ¼ cup flour, baking powder and salt and set aside. Combine remaining sugar and orange peel in processor. Process 10 seconds, until rind is finely chopped. Add 4 tablespoons butter. Process 5 seconds. Add egg. Process 1 second. Add buttermilk and almond extract. Process 3 seconds, until well blended. Add 1 cup flour. Process 3 seconds. Add remaining ¼ cup flour. Pulse 3 to 4 seconds. Turn into skillet over cranberry mixture. Bake in preheated 350° oven for 40 minutes. Turn out immediately onto platter. Serve warm with whipped cream if desired. Makes 6 to 8 servings.

CRANBERRY CATSUP

1 8-ounce can whole-cranberry
    sauce
¼ cup sugar
2 tablespoons cider vinegar, or
    to taste

¾ teaspoon cinnamon
½ teaspoon allspice
¼ teaspoon salt
⅛ teaspoon freshly ground
    pepper

Fit processor with METAL BLADE. Break up cranberry sauce and add to processor with remaining ingredients. Process 7 to 8 seconds. Turn into saucepan and bring to a boil. Reduce heat and simmer, stirring occasionally, 5 minutes, or until mixture is thick. Serve warm or cold. Refrigerate, covered, up to 4 weeks. Makes 1 cup.

GINGER SQUASH CAKE

A good use for leftover winter squash. They'll never guess what's in the cake.

18 gingersnaps, halved
1 teaspoon baking powder
1 cup flour
¾ teaspoon baking soda
¼ teaspoon cloves
½ teaspoon cinnamon
½ cup butter or margarine, cut
    in 1-inch pieces

½ cup brown sugar, packed
2 eggs
¼ cup buttermilk
¾ cup puréed winter squash
Cream Cheese Icing (recipe
    follows)

Fit processor with METAL BLADE. Process gingersnaps 5 seconds until very fine crumbs. (Process half the amount at a time.) Remove to bowl. Combine baking powder with ¼ cup flour and set aside. Combine remaining flour, baking soda and spices with gingersnaps. Put butter and sugar into processor. Process 5 seconds. Add eggs. Process 3 seconds. Add buttermilk and squash. Process 3 seconds. Add gingersnap mixture. Process 3 to 4 seconds. Add reserved flour and baking powder. Pulse 3 to 4 times. A little flour may remain on top. Turn out into greased 9-inch square pan. Bake in preheated 350° oven for 35 to 45 minutes, until cake tests done. When cool, frost with Cream Cheese Icing. Makes 6 to 9 servings.

CREAM CHEESE ICING

1 3-ounce package cream
   cheese, cut in 1-inch cubes
3 tablespoons butter or
   margarine

2 cups confectioners' sugar
1 teaspoon vanilla

Fit processor with METAL BLADE. Combine ingredients and process 15 to 20 seconds, until smooth and well blended. Yield: 1 cup

GRAHAM-ORANGE LAYER CAKE

A cake that is rich in flavor but light as air.

15 graham crackers, broken
1¼ cups pecans
½ teaspoon baking powder
1 cup sugar
Rind of ½ orange, cut in 2-inch-
   long strips

6 eggs, separated
⅓ cup orange juice
2 tablespoons milk
⅓ cup apricot jam, heated
1 cup heavy cream, whipped

Fit processor with METAL BLADE. Process crackers 10 seconds. Remove to bowl. Process nuts 5 seconds. Combine 1 cup nuts with cracker crumbs. Stir in baking powder. Combine sugar and orange rind in processor. Process 20 seconds. Add egg yolks. Process 3 seconds. Add orange juice and milk. Process 3 seconds. Add cracker mixture. Pulse 5 times. Beat whites until stiff. Pour yolk mixture over whites and fold together. Turn into 2 greased and floured 9-inch round cake tins. Bake in preheated 350° oven for 25 minutes. Let stand on racks for 10 minutes. Run knife around edges of pans and turn cake out onto racks. Be careful not to tear cake when removing. When cool, spread with warm jam between layers. Frost top and sides with whipped cream. Decorate with reserved ¼ cup pecans. Serves 8 to 10.

SPICY SQUASH-DATE CAKE

Another use for a surplus crop of butternut squash.

2 cups flour	½ teaspoon allspice
½ cup dates	1 medium butternut squash
½ cup walnuts	1 cup sugar
2 teaspoons baking soda	1 cup brown sugar, packed
1 teaspoon baking powder	4 eggs
2 teaspoons cinnamon	1⅓ cups oil
1 teaspoon ground ginger	Rum Butter Cream (recipe follows)

Combine 2 tablespoons flour with dates and nuts, tossing together. Combine remaining flour, soda, baking powder and spices. Set aside. Using vegetable peeler, peel squash, remove seeds and strings and cut into pieces that will fit into feed tube. Fit processor with SHREDDING DISC. Shred squash. Measure 4 cups and turn into mixing bowl. Refrigerate remainder for another use. Remove SHREDDING DISC. Fit METAL BLADE into bowl. Process dates and nuts by pulsing 4 to 5 times, until chopped. Add to squash. Put sugars, eggs and oil into processor. Pulse 5 to 6 times, until well mixed. Add dry ingredients and process 5 seconds, until well mixed. Turn into mixing bowl and fold all together. Turn into 2 well-greased and floured 9-inch cake pans. Bake in 350° oven for 40 minutes, until cake tests done. Remove pans to rack and cool 10 minutes. Turn out cake onto racks. When thoroughly cool, frost with Rum Butter Cream. This cake may be frozen. Makes 1 9-inch layer cake.

RUM BUTTER CREAM

The flavoring may be changed to suit your taste.

2 egg yolks	4 cups confectioners' sugar
1½ cups butter or margarine, or a combination of both, cut in 1-inch pieces	3 tablespoons rum
	⅓ cup milk

Fit processor with METAL BLADE. Put yolks and shortening into bowl. Process 6 seconds, or until well mixed. Add sugar and process 20 seconds, until well blended. Add rum and milk. Process 5 seconds, until smooth. Makes enough to frost 1 9-inch layer cake.

RITA BANNACK'S ZUCCHINI CHOCOLATE CAKE

A cake for zucchini lovers, and chocolate lovers, and cake lovers in general. It freezes well.

2 pounds zucchini, unpeeled
2 teaspoons salt
1 cup walnuts or pecans
2 cups flour
1 teaspoon baking powder
1 teaspoon baking soda
1 teaspoon cinnamon
½ teaspoon nutmeg
¼ cup cocoa
3 eggs
2 cups sugar
½ cup oil
1 teaspoon vanilla
¾ cup buttermilk

Fit processor with SHREDDING DISC. Cut zucchini into pieces to fit feed tube. Shred and remove to colander. Sprinkle with salt and let stand 30 minutes. Fit processor with METAL BLADE. Process nuts 3 seconds. Remove. Combine ½ cup flour with baking powder and soda. Set aside. Combine remaining flour with spices and cocoa. Squeeze zucchini dry with hands. Add eggs and sugar to processor. Process 2 seconds. Add oil and vanilla. Process 1 second. Add buttermilk. Process 2 seconds. Add flour-cocoa mixture. Process 4 seconds. Add zucchini and nuts. Process 2 seconds. Add remaining ½ cup flour. Pulse 3 to 4 times. Turn into 2 well-greased and floured 9-inch cake tins. Bake in preheated 350° oven for 35-45 minutes, until cake tests done. Cool for 10 minutes. Turn out onto racks. When cool, spread with Cream Cheese Icing (see page 146 for recipe). Sprinkle top with grated chocolate.

RAW APPLE COOKIES

Tasty and nutritious.

1½ cups flour
½ teaspoon each salt, baking powder and baking soda
½ teaspoon each cinnamon and ground cloves
½ cup walnuts
½ cup pitted dates
½ cup raisins
2 large firm apples, cored and cut into chunks, with skin left on
½ cup shortening
1 cup brown sugar, packed
2 eggs
1 cup uncooked quick oats

Combine ½ cup flour with salt, baking powder, baking soda and spices. Set aside. Fit processor with METAL BLADE. Process walnuts 3 seconds. Remove to bowl. Combine dates, raisins and 1 tablespoon flour and process 5 seconds. Add to nuts. Process apple chunks, one apple at a time, 3 to 4 seconds until chopped into small pieces. Remove. Add shortening, sugar and eggs to processor. Process 7 seconds, until well blended. Add oats and 1 cup flour. Process 5 seconds. Add nut mixture. Process 3 seconds. Add apples, remaining ½ cup flour and spice mixture. Pulse 4 to 5 times, until just blended. Turn out into bowl. Drop well-rounded teaspoonfuls 1½–2 inches apart on greased baking sheets. Bake in preheated 350° oven 12 to 15 minutes, or until lightly browned. Remove to rack to cool. Makes 60.

BLUEBERRY-ORANGE SQUARES

A nice combination to go with minted iced tea on a summer day.

½ cup walnuts
1 cup fresh blueberries
Rind of 1 orange, in strips
1 cup flour
1 teaspoon baking powder

½ teaspoon salt
1 cup brown sugar, packed
2 eggs
¼ cup melted butter or
   margarine
1 teaspoon cinnamon

Fit processor with METAL BLADE. Process nuts 3 seconds. Remove to bowl with berries. Remove orange rind with vegetable peeler. Combine ¼ cup flour with baking powder and salt and set aside. Put orange peel and sugar into processor. Process 10 seconds, until orange peel is finely grated. Add eggs and butter. Process 3 seconds. Add remaining ¾ cup flour and cinnamon. Process 4 seconds. Add ¼ cup flour mixture. Pulse 3 times. Turn out into bowl with berries and fold all together. Turn into well-greased 8-inch square baking pan. Bake for 35 to 40 minutes, until cake tests done. Cut into squares while warm. Makes 9 squares.

CHEESECAKE SQUARES

These can be finger-food cheesecake, depending on the size you make them.

½ cup walnuts
¼ cup toasted wheat germ
⅓ cup brown sugar, packed
½ cup whole wheat flour
5 tablespoons butter or
  margarine, cut in ½-inch
  pieces

Rind of 1 lemon, cut in ½-inch
  pieces
½ cup granulated sugar
2 tablespoons vanilla yogurt
1 egg
1 8-ounce package cream cheese

Fit processor with METAL BLADE. Combine nuts, wheat germ, brown sugar and flour in processor. Process 3 seconds. Add butter. Process 3 seconds, until mixture is crumbly. Remove. Measure out one cup and set aside. Press remaining mixture over bottom of 8-inch square baking pan. Bake in preheated 350° oven for 12 minutes. Combine lemon rind and sugar in processor. Process 10 seconds, until rind is finely chopped. Add yogurt, egg and cream cheese. Process 5 seconds, until mixture is smooth. Spread over crust and top with remaining 1 cup crumbs. Bake for 25 minutes. Cool before cutting. Makes 9 large squares, 16 small squares.

A CHRISTMASY COOKIE

Children of all ages love them.

1 cup assorted gumdrops
2 cups flour
½ cup walnuts or pecans

1 cup brown sugar, packed
1 teaspoon vanilla

Fit processor with METAL BLADE. Put gumdrops and 1 tablespoon flour into processor. Process 10 to 15 seconds. Add nuts. Process 10 seconds longer. Gumdrops should be in largish pieces. Add brown sugar, vanilla and remaining flour. Process 5 seconds, until mixture is well blended. Turn into well-greased 8-inch square pan. Bake in 350° oven for 50 to 60 minutes. Cut while warm and remove to racks. Makes 16 squares. Can be frozen.

DREAM BARS

*Correctly named, these cookies are a dream both to
make and to eat.*

Crust:

¼ cup butter or margarine, cut
   in ½-inch pieces
½ cup brown sugar, packed

1 cup flour
½ cup rolled oats

Fit processor with METAL BLADE. Combine butter in processor with sugar.
Process 3 seconds. Add flour and oats. Process 5 seconds. Remove and pat into greased
8 x 8-inch square pan. Bake in 325° oven for 7 minutes. Remove.

Filling:

1 cup walnuts or pecans
1 cup raisins
2 eggs
¾ cup brown sugar, packed

1 teaspoon vanilla
1 teaspoon baking powder
3 tablespoons flour

Fit processor with METAL BLADE. Process nuts and raisins 3 seconds. Remove. Combine eggs, sugar and vanilla. Process 2 seconds. Mix baking powder with flour. Add,
and pulse 3 times. Add nut mixture and process 1 second. Turn into pan, spreading
over crust. Bake in 325° oven for 30 minutes. Cut into bars while warm. Makes 16
bars.

GRANOLA BARS

1⅔ cups granola cereal
¾ cup shredded coconut
1 cup nuts
⅓ cup sesame seed
2 strips orange peel
1½ cups brown sugar, packed
1 cup butter or margarine

2 eggs
1 teaspoon vanilla
1 teaspoon salt
1 teaspoon soda
1¾ cups flour
½ cup wheat germ
½ cup nonfat dry milk

Fit processor with METAL BLADE. Process granola 3 seconds. Remove to large bowl. Process coconut, nuts and sesame seed 3 seconds. Remove to bowl. Process orange peel and sugar 5 seconds. Add butter. Process 4 seconds. Add eggs and vanilla. Process 3 seconds. Combine salt and soda with ¼ cup flour. Set aside. Add remaining flour, wheat germ and dry milk to processor. Process 5 to 6 seconds. Add remaining ¼ cup flour. Pulse 3 or 4 times. Turn out and mix with granola in bowl. Spread mixture in greased 10 x 15-inch baking pan. Bake in 350° oven for 25 to 30 minutes. Cool in pan on rack. Cut into bars. Makes about 3 dozen.

OATMEAL-LEMONADE BARS

Good to have on hand. They freeze well.

Filling:

¾ cup walnuts or other nuts
1 12-ounce package pitted
 prunes
1 6-ounce can frozen lemonade
 concentrate, thawed,
 undiluted

1 lemonade can water
⅓ cup sugar
¼ cup flour
½ teaspoon salt

Fit processor with METAL BLADE. Process nuts 3 seconds. Remove. Process prunes 5 seconds, until chopped. Remove to saucepan. Add lemonade concentrate and water to prunes. Simmer 15 to 20 minutes, until consistency of purée. Stir in remaining ingredients.

Crumb Mixture:

¾ cup butter or margarine, cut
 in ½-inch pieces
1 cup brown sugar, packed
1¾ cups flour

1 teaspoon each baking soda
 and salt
1¾ cups rolled oats

Distribute butter evenly around bowl of processor. Add sugar. Process 6 seconds, until blended. Combine ¼ cup flour with soda and salt. Set aside. Add remaining flour and oats to processor. Process 8 to 10 seconds. Add flour-soda mixture. Pulse 4 or 5 times. Mixture should be crumbly. Press half of crumb mixture into greased 13 x 9 x 2-inch pan. Flatten. Evenly spread on prune filling. Sprinkle with remaining crumb mixture. Pat lightly. Bake in preheated 400° oven for 25 to 30 minutes, or until lightly browned. Cool slightly in pan on rack. Cut in 36 bars and remove from pan to rack to cool completely.

PECAN BUTTONS

*A short, rich little cookie that freezes well and gets
eaten up in a hurry.*

2 cups pecans
1 cup butter or margarine, cut
   in 1-inch pieces
¼ cup brown sugar, packed

2 teaspoons vanilla
2 cups flour
1 cup confectioners' sugar

Fit processor with METAL BLADE. Process nuts, ½ cup at a time, 3 seconds. They should be fairly fine in texture. Remove. Add butter and brown sugar. Process 10 seconds, stopping to scrape batter down from sides. Add vanilla and flour. Process 10 seconds. Add nuts. Process 2 seconds. Roll dough into walnut-size balls and place on baking sheet. Bake in preheated 250° oven for 30 minutes. While still warm, roll in confectioners' sugar. Makes about 3½ dozen.

RAISIN PICNIC BARS

Good to take along in the basket or backpack.

½ cup walnuts
1 cup raisins
½ cup wheat germ
1 cup flour
¾ teaspoon salt
1½ teaspoons baking powder

⅓ cup butter or margarine, cut
   in ½-inch pieces
1¼ cups brown sugar, packed
2 eggs
1 teaspoon vanilla

Fit processor with METAL BLADE. Process walnuts 3 seconds. Remove to small bowl. Add raisins and wheat germ to processor. Process 3 seconds. Add to nuts. Combine ¼ cup flour and salt with baking powder. Set aside. Distribute butter evenly around bowl of food processor. Add sugar. Process 5 seconds. Add eggs and vanilla. Process 4 seconds, until well blended. Add ¾ cup flour. Process 3 seconds. Add nut mixture. Process 2 seconds. Add flour and baking powder mixture. Pulse 3 to 4 times just to mix. Turn out and spread in greased 9-inch square pan. Bake in preheated 350° oven for 25 to 30 minutes. Cool on rack and cut in bars. Makes 18.

PEAR CRUNCH PIE

A special early autumn dessert.

1 unbaked 9-inch pie shell
1 tablespoon apricot or peach
   jam
1 teaspoon water
5 medium ripe pears
1 tablespoon lemon juice

1 cup brown sugar, packed
1½ cups corn flakes
1 teaspoon cinnamon
½ teaspoon ginger
⅓ cup butter or margarine

Place pie shell in preheated 425° oven. Bake for 8 minutes. Meanwhile, heat jam with water until syrupy. Brush pie shell with jam. Return to oven for 2 minutes. Cool. Reduce heat to 375°. Peel, core and slice pears into thin slices. Arrange in pie shell and sprinkle with lemon juice. Fit processor with METAL BLADE. Combine sugar and corn flakes in processor. Process 7 seconds, until finely crushed. Add cinnamon, ginger and butter. Process 5 seconds, until crumbly. Spread over pears. Bake 45 to 50 minutes, until pears are tender and top is crisp. Serve warm with ice cream if desired. Makes 6 servings.

ORANGE-SCENTED APPLE CRUMB PIE

A natural for the processor, which makes short work
of pastry, filling and topping.

Pastry:
½ cup solid vegetable
   shortening
4 tablespoons butter or
   margarine, or half each, cut in
   1-inch pieces

2½ cups flour
3 tablespoons frozen orange
   juice concentrate

Fit processor with METAL BLADE. Add shortening and butter and process 2 seconds. Add flour and orange juice and process 20 to 30 seconds, until dough starts to make a ball around spindle. Remove and wrap. Chill at least 30 minutes. Divide in half. Roll out half of dough and fit into 9-inch pie pan. Bake in preheated 425° oven for 8 minutes. Cool.

Filling:

5 medium-size tart apples,
cored, peeled and cut in
quarters

¾ cup sugar
2 tablespoons flour

Fit processor with SLICING DISC. Slice apples. Turn into bowl and mix with sugar and flour. Fill pastry-lined pan.

Topping:

½ cup butter or margarine
½ cup brown sugar, packed
1 teaspoon cinnamon

½ cup flour
½ cup walnuts
Grated rind of ½ orange

Fit processor with METAL BLADE. Combine all ingredients and process for 10 seconds. Spread topping over apples. Place pie pan on baking sheet. Bake in 400° oven for 40 minutes. Serve warm with a spoonful of orange yogurt or softly whipped cream. Makes 6 to 8 servings.

STRAWBERRY-CHEESE PIE

*A crust of dates and oats makes this pie a bit
different. It also freezes well.*

Pastry:

1 cup pitted dates
1 cup rolled oats

3 tablespoons shortening

Fit processor with METAL BLADE. Process dates for 4 seconds. Pulse 2 or 3 times. Add oats and shortening. Process for 2 to 3 seconds, until mixture is fairly smooth. Press into 8-inch pie pan. Freeze while preparing filling.

Filling:

2 strips orange peel, 2 x ½
inches
½ cup sugar
8-ounce package cream cheese,
cut in 1-inch pieces
1 egg

1 10-ounce package frozen
strawberries, thawed
½ teaspoon almond extract or 1
tablespoon orange liqueur
1 cup sour cream

Fit processor with METAL BLADE. Process orange peel with sugar 10 seconds, or until finely chopped. Replace METAL BLADE with PLASTIC BLADE. Add cream cheese, egg and ¼ cup strawberry juice. Process for 5 seconds. Add flavoring. Process 1 second. Turn into prepared crust. Bake in preheated 350° oven 30 minutes, until set. Spread with sour cream. Bake 10 minutes longer. Cool. Spread strawberries over top. Makes 6 servings.

VERMONT APPLE PIE

A special pie with the true flavor of New England, to eat warm with wedges of sharp cheddar cheese.

Pastry:
¾ cup shortening, cut in
  chunks
2 cups flour
½ cup walnuts

½ teaspoon salt
3 tablespoons apple juice
  concentrate

Fit processor with METAL BLADE. Place shortening around bowl of processor. Add flour, walnuts and salt. Process 10 seconds. Add concentrate and process until dough forms a ball around spindle. If dough is too dry, add a little more liquid. Remove, wrap and chill.

Filling:
6 medium tart apples, peeled,
  cored and quartered
¾ cup sugar

3 tablespoons flour
2 ounces sharp cheddar cheese
¼ cup maple syrup

Fit processor with SLICING DISC. Slice apples and turn into bowl. Toss with sugar and flour. Fit processor with SHREDDING DISC. Shred cheese. Divide pastry in half. Roll out half and fit into 9-inch pie pan. Fill with half of apple mixture. Sprinkle cheese over apples. Top with remaining apples. Drizzle maple syrup over all. Roll out remaining pastry and fit over top. Seal edges. Prick top with fork. Place pan on baking sheet. Bake in preheated 425° oven for 10 minutes. Reduce heat to 400° and bake for 40 minutes, until pie is bubbling. Serve warm. Makes 8 servings.

Equivalents

Apple, 1 medium	chopped	½ cup
	sliced	¾ cup
Avocado, 1 medium	puréed	½–¾ cup
Beef, ½ pound, boneless	ground	1 cup
Bread, 1 slice	crumbed	½ cup
Cabbage, ½ medium head	shredded	5 cups
Carrots, 1 medium	sliced	½ cup
Cheese: cheddar, 4 ounces	shredded	1 cup
—— Parmesan, 4 ounces	grated	1¼ cups
Chicken, ½ pound, boneless	ground	1 cup
Cucumber, 1 medium	sliced	1¼ cups
Mushrooms, 4 ounces	chopped	1¼ cups
	sliced	1¼ cups
Onions, 1 medium	chopped	½ cup
	sliced	1 cup
Pepper, 1 medium	chopped	1 cup
	sliced	1 cup
Potatoes, 1 medium	shredded	½ cup
	sliced	¾ cup
Zucchini, 1 medium	chopped	1½ cups
	shredded	1 cup
	sliced	1½ cups

INDEX